Pole $_t^{}$ / Pole $_0^{}$

THE PHOTOGRAPHS

Pole

Pole

THE PHOTOGRAPHS

BY BASIL PAO • TEXT BY MICHAEL PALIN

ALL PHOTOGRAPHS BY **BASIL PAO**
EXCEPT PAGES 8 / 9, 11, 13 (TOP) BY
FRASER BARBER, PAGE 12 BY
PATTI MUSICARO, AND PAGES 190 /
191 BY **NIGEL MEAKIN**.

PUBLISHED BY **BBC BOOKS**,
A DIVISION OF BBC ENTERPRISES LTD.,
WOODLANDS, 80 WOOD LANE,
LONDON W12 0TT
FIRST PUBLISHED 1994

PHOTOGRAPHS © BASIL PAO, 1994
TEXT © MICHAEL PALIN, 1994
THE MORAL RIGHT OF THE
AUTHORS HAS BEEN ASSERTED.

ISBN 0 563 37018 1

DTP ARTIST : LUI SZE SHING,
PETER WONG DESIGN & ASSOCIATES
TYPOGRAPHY : HEADLINES SET IN
50 AND 20PT GARAMOND 3,
BODYTEXT IN 14 AND 10 PT
GARAMOND 3 BY MACINTOSH IIFX.

COLOUR SEPARATION BY SAKAI
LITHOCOLOUR CO., LTD. HONG KONG
PRINTED & BOUND IN GREAT BRITAIN
BY BUTLER & TANNER LTD., FROME
JACKET PRINTED BY LAWRENCE
ALLEN LTD., WESTON-SUPER-MARE

CONTENTS

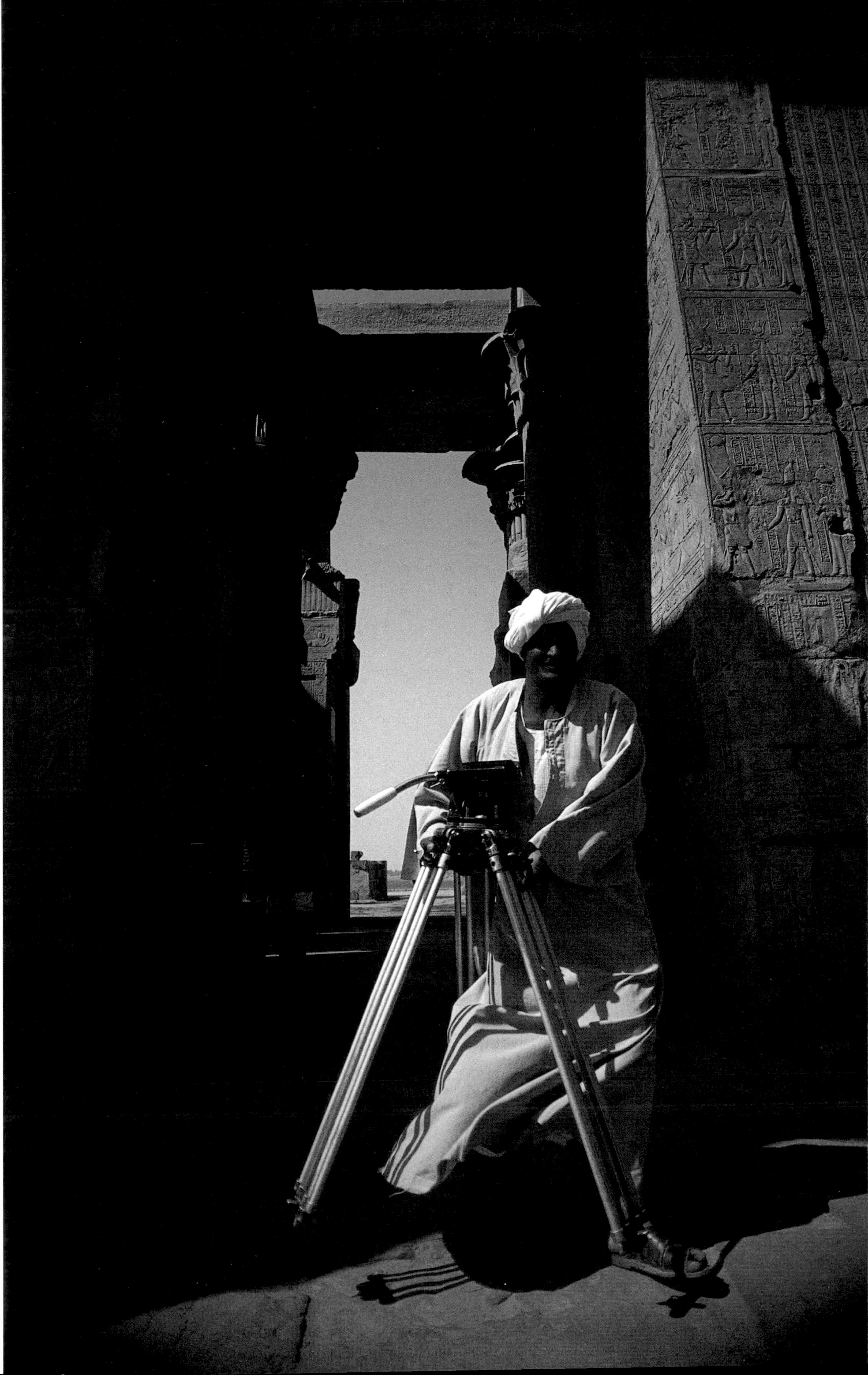

FOREWORD

THERE WILL NEVER be another journey like Pole to Pole – so easy on paper and so hard on sand, rock, water and ice. I was ready for anything but not for everything. How could I have been? How do you prepare for 17 countries and 23,000 miles (37,000 kilometres) of travel in less than half a year? My shopping list included – two Poles, two Tropics, one Equator, assorted ice-packs, glaciers, deltas, deserts, waterfalls, swamps, pyramids, temples, craters, hippos, penguins, rapids, mineshafts and mud; Europe's third longest river, the world's longest river, temperatures of 50 Celsius above and 50 Celsius below. And that was without the people. All those I met and watched and worked with and wondered at in 71 different stop-overs. Much of the time this stupendous journey, this once-in-a-lifetime traveller's dream, was experienced in a blur of fatigue, with bodies weary from the physical demands of filming, senses numbed by hostile climates and minds preoccupied with lower things – where to eat, what to eat, and what to do with what you've eaten once you've eaten it.

The only hope was that somebody in the seven-strong party was awake when you were sleeping or strong when you were weak, or adventurous when everyone else was playing safe, or curious when no one else wanted to know. That somebody was as often as not Basil Pao, our stills photographer. On a bad day he was as incurious and unadventurous as any of us, but whilst the rest of the crew shot film and recorded sound for the series and I scribbled in my notebook and walked and talked for the series, Basil was free to look around, to point his camera wherever he wanted (frequently getting himself into trouble as he did so), in short, to look at the extraordinary worlds we passed through with a fresh, enquiring, free-roving eye. Like all of us he sometimes suffered from lack of appetite and sheer sensory overload, but there weren't many days during those five and a half months when his camera stayed in his bag.

Two hundred and fifty of his pictures appeared in the original *Pole to Pole* book. Over thirty thousand didn't, which is what this book is about.

Anyone who saw the Hong Kong and Chinese leg of *Around the World in Eighty Days* will know Basil Pao and anyone who has seen the photos that accompanied it will know that he is a sensationally good photographer. This time I was not going to make the mistake of leaving him behind for any of the journey, and as soon as I saw his photos, his design and layout for *Pole to Pole – The Photographs* I know it was one of the best decisions I ever made.

This is the world – from Pole to Pole – as I want to remember it.

Michael Palin. London

NORTH POLE

Svalbard, Norway & Finland

TO HELSINKI

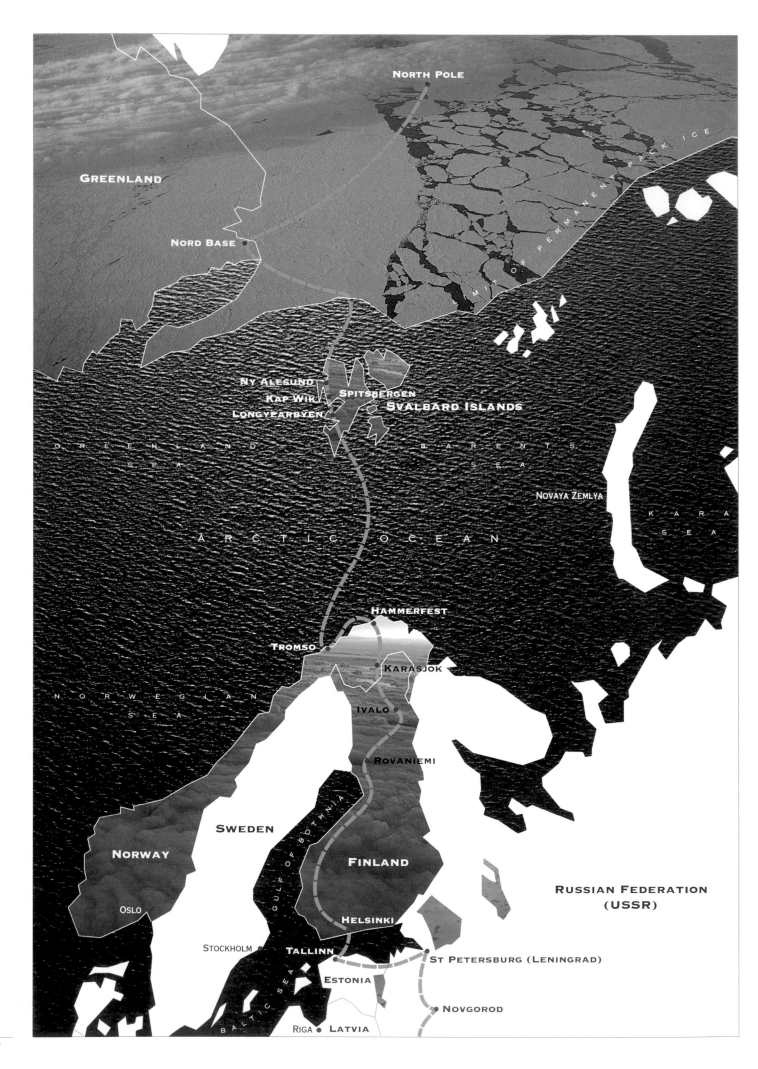

NORTH POLE

GREENLAND

NORD BASE

LIMIT OF PERMANENT PACK ICE

NY ALESUND
KAP WIK   SPITSBERGEN
LONGYEARBYEN   SVALBARD ISLANDS

GREENLAND
SEA

BARENTS
SEA

NOVAYA ZEMLYA

KARA
SEA

ARCTIC OCEAN

HAMMERFEST

TROMSO

KARASJOK

NORWEGIAN
SEA

IVALO

ROVANIEMI

SWEDEN

GULF OF BOTHNIA

NORWAY

FINLAND

RUSSIAN FEDERATION
(USSR)

OSLO

HELSINKI

STOCKHOLM

TALLINN

ST PETERSBURG (LENINGRAD)

ESTONIA

NOVGOROD

BALTIC SEA

RIGA   LATVIA

NORTH POLE TO HELSINKI
Svalbard, Norway & Finland

(ABOVE) **Setting out from 90 degrees North. There is no North Pole. You have to bring your own.**

(PRECEDING PAGES) **Cameraman Nigel Meakin sets up his own television station in the pack ice of the Greenland Sea.**

ESCENDING to the North Pole was a test of fear and faith. I'm glad I got to know both so early in the journey. We arrived at the Pole in our tight-packed, over-crowded De Havilland Twin-Otter only to find the ice breaking up beneath us after an unusually mild winter. Twice we tried to put down on an ice-floe, twice we pulled away at the last minute; twice my heart reached my mouth, and only after circling almost an hour did we touch down on the roof of the world at the third attempt. I was tempted to call it third time lucky, but I didn't like to think too much of luck, preferring to believe only in the experience and judgement of our veteran pilot. As we plunged down towards the broken ice and streaming black water of the Arctic Ocean, I only felt confident when I could actually see him. I've rarely been able to say that my fate rested entirely on someone else's shoulders, but on *Pole to Pole* it happened more often than I care to admit.

My relief at reaching the Svalbard Islands, was tempered by the terrifying beauty of the place where we had landed – the island of Spitsbergen, where an all-year ice-cap and frequent snow-storms concealed jagged outcrops and plunging crevasses. From this inhospitable point

Svalbard Islands

(ABOVE) Journey through the Ice Age: On motor-sledges crossing the glaciers and heading into ice-walled ravines on the island of Spitsbergen. Believe it or not, we passed reindeer and Arctic fox, both of which somehow scrape a living out of this.

(FAR RIGHT) Roald Amundsen: first man on the South Pole (December 1911), stares longingly southwards from Tromso.

onwards we forsook aircraft for snow scooters. The two day journey across the magnificent glacial wilderness of North Spitsbergen was as rigorous as any of the next 23,000 miles (37,000 kilometres) and as rewarding. We were travelling through the Ice Age.

Our route to the South Pole was to follow, as far as possible, the 30 degrees East meridian – the line of longitude which crossed most land and least water. But in the Arctic there are few options. You go where it's safe.

We did not finally leave the ice behind until we reached the Barents Sea. Our escape route from the frozen North was the small, sturdy M.V. *Norsel* which pushed aside the ice with ease but bobbed like a cork once she hit the open sea. But she brought us safe to the northern portals of Europe, dramatic sheer-sided fiords – friendly havens for sailors but impenetrable barriers for land travellers.

We thawed out at Tromso, still way north of the Arctic Circle, but the first place where we could relax the anxious vigilance which is the characteristic of travel in extreme climates. Man is not meant to live much further north than this, and if he chooses to, then he must face not only the inevitable physical discomfort but the mental concentration required to stay alive and well and safe. Tromso is the northernmost and friendliest of cities. Doors are not locked, strangers are welcome. "No one will answer the door here," I was told..."because they expect you to walk in."

With its own brewery, university, cathedral, cafés and Chinese restaurants, Tromso was the only place that tempted us to linger in the Arctic. But, taking inspiration from the tall figure of Roald Amundsen, whose statue looks soulfully southwards, to that tiny, significant

point of the earth which he was the first human being to discover, we moved on - mentally if not physically, in his footsteps.

Progress is not easy across Northern Scandinavia. The hard terrain of the Finnmark Plateau has barely been touched by the road builders and much of the local transport is on coastal ships which weave their way through the off-shore islands.

The ship took me to Hammerfest, the world's most northerly town, from which a car took me southwards, by road, across the hard, bleak, windswept shield we know as Lapland, only to discover there is no Lapland and no Lapps. The nomadic people who have moved herds of reindeer across these inaccessible northlands for thousands of years prefer to call themselves the Same ("Sar-mi"), and in Karasjok, Norway, they even have their own Same Parliament building.

This is a quiet land of lakes, conifers and monster mosquitoes. A good metalled road known as the Arctic Highway slices through it across the border into Finland. At the town of Rovaniemi we reached our first railway line. In one overnight train journey we finally left the North behind. Helsinki was as warm as the Mediterranean, and we experienced nocturnal darkness for the first time for more than three weeks.

Helsinki, with its neo-classical buildings mirroring the great city of St. Petersburg 180 miles (290 kilometres) away across the Bay of Finland, was soft and comforting. Suddenly food was plentiful - the fish and vegetables and fruit were stacked on market stalls in lavish profusion. The city was clean, well-kept, proud of itself, but fearful of its success. Fearful, more than anything, that its relatively strong economy would provide a ready job market for the unemployed of its giant neighbour, Russia. Especially fearful in that extraordinary summer of 1991, when the old Soviet Union was as unpredictable as it had ever been.

Tromso

(ABOVE) The world's most
northerly city, 200 miles
(320 kilometres) above the
Arctic Circle. Summertime
is short but spectacular.
Once out, the sun doesn't
set for three months.
(RIGHT) Midnight in Tromso.
(TOP) Interior of the Arctic
Cathedral. (FAR RIGHT)
Round-the-clock thirst is
slaked by Mack Beer,
produce of the world's
most northerly Brewery.

Karasjok

In what we shouldn't call Lapland, the people who aren't called Lapps dance in the midnight sun. The costume is traditional Same (pronounced *Sar-mi*), the music a curious form of chanting called the Joik. (LEFT) The Arctic hots up. A wedding party at the Cormorant Restaurant in Tromso.

Karasjok

(TOP LEFT) Now that the Arctic Highway has opened up the frozen north to tourists, the nomadic Same paradoxically move less. Reindeer, in its various forms, still remains a source of income.

(BOTTOM LEFT) Johan and Anne-Marie Anders: last of the reindeer farmers?

(LEFT & ABOVE) The vivid colours of the Same dress and the intricate gold and silver of their ornaments have not changed for centuries, but today's nomads keep in touch by portable telephone and canoe rides up the Karasjok River are motor-assisted.

(PRECEDING PAGES) Only the older generation of Same can remember the days when their reindeer herds were all that moved across the inhospitable Finnmark Plateau.

Helsinki

(LEFT & RIGHT) Because they see so little of it, the Finns adore heat and sunshine. There are five million people in Finland and almost as many lakes, so nearly everyone has their own pool.

(ABOVE) Forging the new Finland. Less than a hundred years after independence the Finns built up the second most prosperous economy in Europe.

The neo-classical heart of Helsinki, especially the Lutheran Cathedral (LEFT & RIGHT), reflects the Russian and Swedish influences of the eighteenth and nineteenth centuries which twentieth century architects like Saarinen tried to get away from with their own National Romantic Style. (TOP) The result is nowhere more impressive than at the Central Station, featuring gods, legends, local wood, stone and copper.

TALLINN

TO ODESSA

Estonia, Russia, Belarus & Ukraine

SWEDEN

FINLAND

HELSINKI

BALTIC SEA

GULF OF FINLAND

St Petersburg (Leningrad)

TALLINN

ESTONIA

NOVGOROD

DNO

RIGA

LATVIA

RUSSIAN FEDERATION
(USSR)

MOSCOW

LITHUANIA

VILNIUS

ORSHA

SMOLENSK

MINSK

BELARUS

ZHLOBIN

WARSAW •

POLAND

CHERNOBYL

NARODICHI

DNIEPER

KIEV

KHARKOV

UKRAINE

SLOVAKIA

CERKASSY

HUNGARY

MOLDOVA

ROSTOV-NA-DONU

ROMANIA

ODESSA

SEA OF AZOV

BUCHAREST •

CRIMEA

KRASNODAR

SEVASTOPOL

YUGOSLAVIA

BLACK SEA

BULGARIA

GREECE

ISTANBUL

TURKEY

THE ESTONIANS and the Finns have always regarded their neighbours as Russians first and Soviets second. In Helsinki and Tallinn it was always "the Russians" they talked of – obsessively and generally contemptuously. They were mistrusted in everything and blamed for everything. But whereas in the last 70 years the Finns had avoided Russian domination and diligently constructed a prosperous capitalist economy the Estonians, sold out by the Germans in 1940, deported en masse by Stalin in the next few years, had been sucked into the Soviet bloc. Their trade turned east towards Moscow, and Russian troops occupied their country, with the result that our short journey across the Gulf of Finland from Helsinki to Tallinn offered a painful contrast. Helsinki Port buzzed with life, Tallinn's dockside was rusting and idle. Helsinki was open and welcoming, Tallinn tight and suspicious. But once past the baleful stare of the security forces, and into the centre of town, the pleasures of the Estonian capital revealed themselves, all the more satisfying for being so well hidden.

Old Tallinn is a delightful, extensive and well-preserved medieval trading city. Though it seemed physically untouched by recent history, we saw by the old city walls huge boulders at the main intersections, put into place in the spring of 1991 when the Estonians feared a Russian crackdown, as had happened to their independence-seeking Lithuanian

Tallinn

Our footfall in what was then the Soviet Union: within two months this was independent Estonia – one of the world's smallest countries (1.5 million people). But the massive Russian Orthodox Cathedral remains, as does a large and awkward percentage of Russian speaking settlers.

Estonia & Russia

(TOP LEFT) **Pride of Tallinn:
The 14th Century Town
Hall in Raekoja Square
took 30 years to build. *Old
Tom*, weather vane and
national symbol, has stood
on top of the tower for 450
years.** (RIGHT) **St. Petersburg
Baroque: 300 years
younger than Tallinn. Peter
The Great used French and
Italian architects to create
his super-city.** (ABOVE) **One
of the attractions of
Novgorod – The Kissing
Dance.**

neighbours. By the summer of '91 political tension was running high in this Hans Christian Andersen world of peaked gables and cobbled streets.

But caution was the watchword, and self-determination was considered to be many years away. The most vigorous manifestation of an enterprise economy was the much discussed activity of the Russian Mafia – running drugs, arms and prostitution rings between Estonia and the West – a grim twist on the old trading relationship which so enriched the city in the middle ages.

Elated and depressed by Estonia, we moved on across the border to Russia and another chapter of frustration and exhilaration.

This huge epic, heroic country was belittled by a swarm of trivial, persistent and apparently self-imposed limitations. The living was not easy. Half-empty hotels had to be booked well in advance. Shopping was not as anywhere else, a simple matter of exchanging goods for money. The rouble itself was worthless and endless coupons and permits were required to buy essentials. After a morning at the shops you were likely to be a gibbering wreck, and if you were looking forward to recovering over a square meal in a restaurant then you were likely to end up a basket case.

Russia is as full of doormen as is Park Avenue in New York. Doors are only opened and tables chosen and food magically produced if you have the right connections. The system of influence and contacts is known as *blat*. For three weeks our Russian escorts worked tirelessly to prove that their *blat* was better than anyone else's. This didn't ensure luxury. It ensured survival.

As in Tallinn, so in the rest of the Soviet Union, the pleasures of life were often beneath the surface. Leningrad (shortly to become St. Petersburg again), is a majestic city but the memories that stick are of women in floral aprons driving trams, priests anointing the knees of men in rolled-up trousers, Sunday tea and talk with a model-maker whose table cloth was a map of the world but who had never in his life been allowed to leave the Soviet Union.

But at least we were back on course. Leningrad/St. Petersburg lay almost astride the 30 degree meridian, as, conveniently, did the two great Ukrainian cities – Kiev and Odessa. Our

route from the Baltic to the Black Sea was that taken by the Vikings ten centuries ago – across the steppes and down the wide, fertile plains of the Dnieper.

We travelled mainly by trains which were always full and friendly. We saw reminders of the rich Russian past – from the golden onion domes of the churches of Novgorod to the massive and heroic military memorials of battles which changed the course of the Second World War.

O utside Kiev the most chilling memorial of all is not to the sacrifices of the past, but the follies of the present. It is the embalmed core of the Number 2 reactor at Chernobyl, the site of the world's worst nuclear accident. For 19 miles (30 kilometres) around it there is an exclusion zone and 19 miles (30 kilometres) beyond that are towns and villages – some deserted – and others inexplicably still waiting to be evacuated. Either no one knows, or no one dares to say how serious are the long-term effects of the massive leaks of radiation. One recent estimate, by a team of Japanese scientists, was that it could be 700 years before the land will be safe again.

The irony is that the countryside round Chernobyl looks to be in the bloom of rude health; the sort of comfortable mix of fields and hedgerows, woodland and wild flowers with which calendars tantalise the tired city dweller. The devastation is invisible, until you look into the dull eyes of those who wait to be moved away, and you look at the dull work of schoolchildren who can no longer draw straight lines or concentrate for more than one hour at a time. We stayed some time in Kiev, an impressive and resilient city which has weathered two human catastrophes – Stalinist collectivisation and Nazi occupation and only narrowly avoided a third because the wind was blowing from the south on the day Chernobyl exploded 55 miles (88 kilometres) away.

As if invigorated by this stroke of good fortune, the capital city of the Ukraine is determined to show an optimistic face – the streets and avenues are clean and well-kept, newly-planted trees and high-spouting fountains alleviate the monumental Stalinist architecture, there are sidewalk cafés and the best night-life we experienced in the Soviet Union. All the talk was of nationalism and yet, as in the Baltic states, even the fiercest patriots were playing it down. "Maybe..." was the key-word..."Maybe... in 40 or 50 years".

From the wide urban spaces of Kiev wide waterways and huge, un-harvested plains led down through Ukraine to the shores of the Black Sea at Odessa. Here was a southern warmth, a southern look to the people; more strolling, less hurrying, good French bread and despite Gorbachev's best efforts to eradicate supply, local red wine. There was also an indefinable shadiness just below the surface. Drunks and streetwalkers. Cries in the night.

Little did we know as we sailed out of Odessa Port on the *Junost*, a training-ship turned ferry boat, that the mighty Soviet Union, the fear of which had shaped and conditioned international affairs throughout our lives, was tottering on the verge of collapse and that, even before we left our next destination – Istanbul – it would have been irreparably wounded by the generals' coup.

Our journey from Helsinki to Odessa passed through one country – the U.S.S.R. On the 26 December 1991 this ceased to exist. The same journey now would pass through four countries: Estonia, Russia, Belarus and Ukraine.

Russia & Ukraine

(LEFT) The onion domes of Novgorod – the city where Russia was founded. Dozens of ancient churches co-exist uneasily with cement works and shabby housing blocks. (ABOVE) Casualties of Chernobyl. The contents of a hastily abandoned maternity clinic in the village of Nozdrische, 45 miles (72 kilometres) from the reactor, are left to decay.

Tallinn

Shadows of old glories. The cobbled streets and plaster walls of medieval Tallinn are rich, extensive, well-preserved and very walkable. They're also a nagging reminder to the grim present of the golden days of Baltic trade.

Tallinn

(ABOVE) **MTV videos and single Russian girls share the early morning hours in the Skybar Disco of the Palace Hotel.**
(LEFT & RIGHT) **In the dressing rooms and hallways backstage, the dancers of Revalia Cabaret ready themselves for the only show in town. Songs and sex for Finnish tourists and Russian families on holiday.**

Tallinn

**The real and the romantic:
Life on the streets is less
heroic but much more
interesting than life on the
monuments.**

St. Petersburg

It's traditional in Russia and much of Eastern Europe to be photographed on your wedding day beside your local monuments. Getting married must be particularly exhausting in St. Petersburg - the choice is endless.

(TOP) Canoodling at the Hermitage. (ABOVE) Cruising past the Battleship *Aurora*. (RIGHT) Laying floral tribute to the well-known despot and city hero: Peter the Great. (FAR RIGHT) Bridal Baroque. The two behind can't make their minds up. The bollards are just good friends.

Faces of Russia's second city. (RIGHT) **Which way now? Impersonator and city guide Alexander Godkov reminds me that when we passed through the city, it still belonged to Lenin.**

St. Petersburg

Religion, sex and satire; officially disapproved of but never eliminated in Russia. (FAR LEFT) A Russian orthodox priest does brisk business with total immersion baptisms in the crypt of the Nevsky Monastery. (ABOVE) Edward Bersudsky, kinematic sculptor. Over the last 15 years he has constructed elaborate and subversive machines with names like "The Big Idea", without anyone understanding them well enough to stop him. (LEFT) Wall decoration: Novgorod-Kiev Express, the train chief's compartment.

Friends and fellow
travellers on the route
south. A Russian punk at
Dno Station. Our train
chief to Kiev. Folk
groups and film makers at
Novgorod. Farmers near
Cerkassy. War veterans at
Odessa.

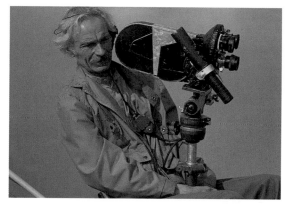

Kiev

A city of memorials: (TOP) Massive suspension bridge over the mighty Dnieper. (TOP RIGHT) Gun barrels on a Second World War memorial – 700,000 citizens were killed or deported by the Nazis – confront the biggest woman I saw in Russia. Over 330 feet (100 metres) high, built on Brezhnev's orders in 1976. She is popularly known by the Ukrainians as *Brezhnev's Mother*. (RIGHT) Past and future in the main square – young Ukrainian cools off in the civic fountains. (FAR RIGHT) Boris Antonienko plays heart-rending Ukrainian folk-songs to tearful audiences.

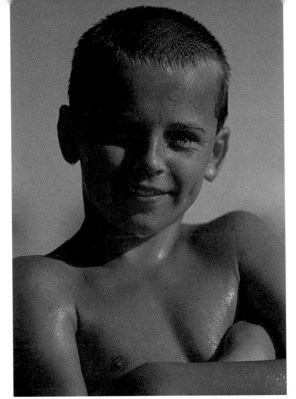

**The Russians swim
enthusiastically anywhere,
even in the Black Sea, so
polluted around its north
coast that an entire
section – the Sea of Azov,
125 miles (200 kilometres)
east – has been completely
closed to bathers.**

Odessa

Ancient marine deposits make the Odessan mud highly prized as a relief for practically everything, especially arthritis. You can take it yourself (RIGHT & TOP LEFT) as this lady doctor did on the beach or (MIDDLE & ABOVE LEFT) have it personally applied by the expert, beefy staff of the Kuyalnik Sanatorium.

Odessa

(LEFT & TOP) Street girls in Odessa. The city fills with tourists during the summer, coming down from the colder north of Russia for sun and fun beside the Black Sea.

(ABOVE) Leaving Odessa: When we left Odessa, with the hammer and sickle of the Soviet Union still dominant, the saddest thing was the sight of those who couldn't come with us. There's something especially poignant about leaving a closed country. Couples may be separated for years; some may never see each other again.

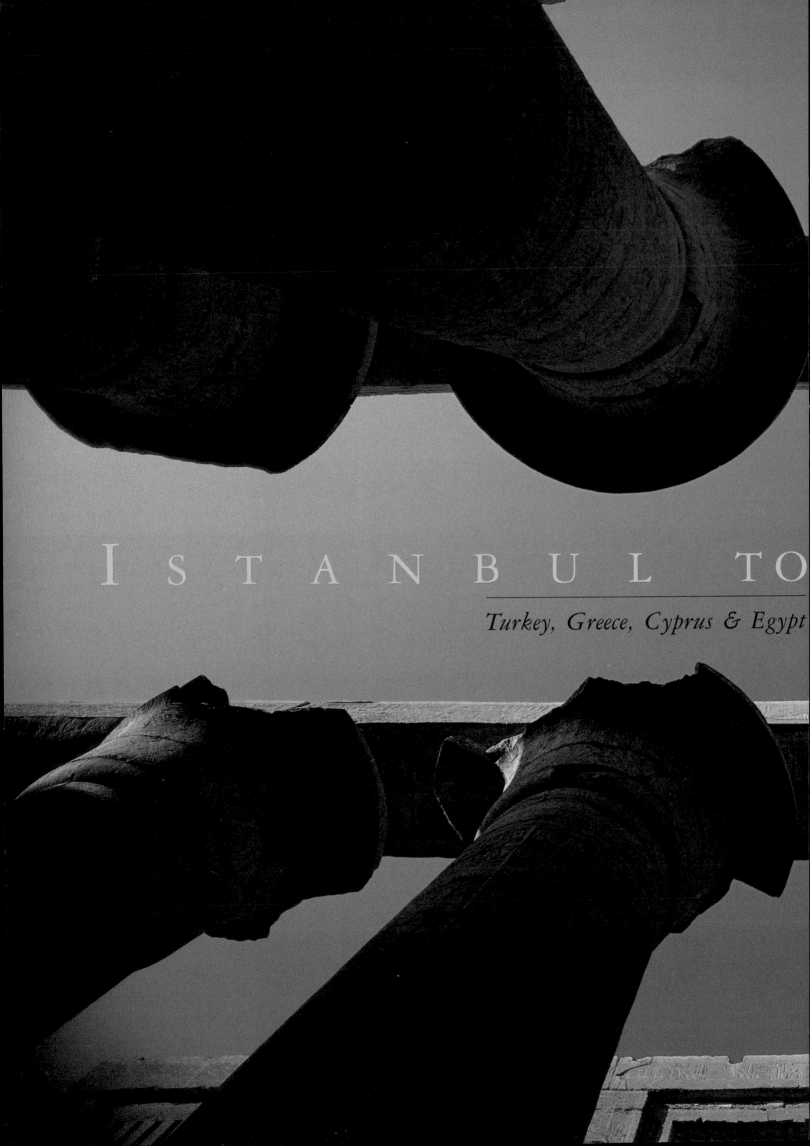

ISTANBUL TO

Turkey, Greece, Cyprus & Egypt

A S W A N

BULGARIA

GREECE

BLACK SEA

ISTANBUL

BANDIRMA

BALIKESIR

Ankara

TURKEY

IZMIR
EPHESUS

ATHENS

MARMARIS

RHODES
LINDOS

SEA OF CRETE

CRETE

CYPRUS

NICOSIA

PAPHOS

LIMASSOL

SYRIA

LEBANON

BEIRUT

DAMASCUS

MEDITERRANEAN SEA

HAIFA

ISRAEL

GAZA

JERUSALEM

PORT SAID

JORDAN

ALEXANDRIA

PETRA

SUEZ CANAL

EL GÎZA
CAIRO

SINAI

GULF OF SUEZ

SAUDI ARABIA

BENI MAZAR

EL MINYA

MALLAWI

ASYUT

WESTERN
DESERT

N
I
L
E

LIBYA

EGYPT

LUXOR

RED SEA

ISNA

ASWAN

ASWAN DAM

TROPIC OF CANCER

LAKE NASSER

ABU SIMBEL

WADI HALFA

SUDAN

STATION 5

STATION 6

ISTANBUL TO ASWAN

ISTANBUL TO ASWAN
Turkey, Greece, Cyprus & Egypt

Luxor

(PRECEDING PAGES & ABOVE) In the Hypostyle Hall at the Temple of Karnak. A forest of columns built to placate the Gods 3,000 years ago. The single most impressive building I saw in five and a half months of travel.

STANBUL is one of the great crossroads of the world. It lies at the southern end of the narrow channel of the Bosporus, linking North and South through the Black Sea and the Mediterranean, East and West via the bridges between Europe and Asia. It is the only city in the world built on two continents. A strong sense of the past, of the continuity of history, fills the place. Roman walls, built in the days when Istanbul was Constantinople, capital of the Eastern Empire, thread their way through the old city; the remains of a Hippodrome lie beside the colossal mosques built by the Ottoman Empire. Urbane shopping arcades and sophisticated hotels testify to the growing links with Western Europe at the end of the nineteenth century. And it's still changing, still adapting. In recent years the influx of Asian, Moslem Turks has doubled the city's population. Facilities have been further stretched by thousands of transients from the rapidly imploding communist countries of Eastern Europe.

After the Soviet Union with its sparse economy and crafty, creative people, Turkey brought us well and truly back to the flesh-pots, offering a brief respite in which to enjoy the benefits of civilisation - honey for breakfast, beer at a café, a dip in a swimming pool, a bath and massage "fit for a sultan", before bending to the task of crossing the Eastern

Mediterranean. Despite the region's ancient traditions of commerce and communication – from the Phoenicians to the Venetians – this proved unexpectedly difficult.

P art of the problem was that the old empires are still scrapping – especially the Turks and Greeks, and neither side will help the other. After we had crossed Asian Turkey to the shores of the Aegean we were faced with gloriously clear jade-green sea and a boat that would take us only as far as Rhodes. (Rhodes being a Greek island, Turks were only allowed to travel there with return tickets.) We reached Rhodes, ate the best meal of the journey so far, and transferred to a cruise liner carrying Israelis to Haifa, which stopped off, conveniently, at the port of Limassol in the divided island of Cyprus, where we picked up a cruise liner bound for Port Said. We were now travelling in the full heat of summer and the icebergs and glaciers we'd left behind never seemed more attractive.

My sense of purpose faltered as we entered a world of holidaymakers and summer visitors, none of them interested in going too far, too fast. They wanted to see the Pyramids, or the birth place of Aphrodite or the temple at Ephesus and then be taken home.

I was tempted to join them. In this Sargasso Sea of sun and sand I found it increasingly hard to remember the clear waters of my original objective. What on earth was I doing, committing myself to months of arduous and unpredictable travel with my wife, family and warm bed only 3 hours' flying time away? Then I would remind myself that these Mediterranean islands were also the home of Ulysses and that perhaps I was part of an older tradition than the package holiday.

I entered Africa in the company of 500 sun-scorched British tourists, not with a bang but a succession of ominous whimpers – equipment dropped in the Mediterranean, customs formalities lasting several hours and Port Said a dry city.

Egypt, with 96 per cent of its land area uninhabitable and its entire burgeoning population

58

confined to the narrow shaft and delta of the Nile, feels crowded and chaotic. This can be intoxicating or irritating according to your fancy. I happen to like the Arab world with its mixture of the stimulating and strident, sensual and secretive. For the foreseeable future our success or failure was firmly linked to it, as we moved south down the longest river in the world – the Nile.

The Nile, rising from two sources in the far-distant mountains of Central Africa, is the fountain of life for the great desert countries of Egypt and the Sudan, where rain hardly ever falls. Only the waters from Ethiopia and Uganda sustain a modern city like Cairo, with a population of around 12 million people. Three thousand years ago they sustained a civilisation as sophisticated and in many ways even more inventive. The great halls I saw at the Temple of Karnak in Luxor demonstrated the breathtaking ingenuity of the Ancient Egyptians, as the richly decorated tombs of the Valley of the Kings on the opposite bank demonstrated their fabulous wealth.

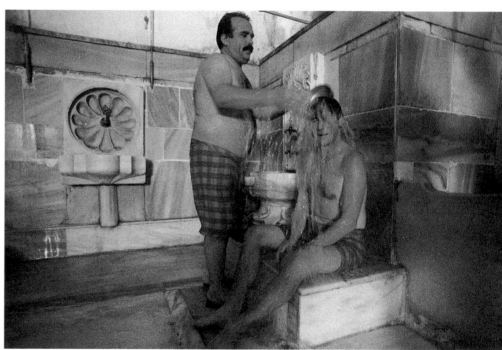

The first 500 miles (800 kilometres) of the great river can be enjoyed in considerable comfort. No previous exploring experience is necessary to cope with a Nile cruise. On an undemanding diet of party games and temple tours we sailed down to Aswan.

Here the carpet ended, and Africa became suddenly less amenable. The tourists and holidaymakers we had travelled with from Istanbul turned back, flew north and west, impatient to be home. Our route to the South Pole now lay through a country which we were strongly advised not to visit. I remember looking out over another smouldering desert sunset and thinking that here at Aswan is where the journey really begins. From here on there could be no turning back.

Istanbul

On well-trodden paths in a landmark city. After the markets (FAR LEFT) a refresher course in the marble chambers of the Cagaloglu Hammam, (ABOVE) the oldest baths in town; buckets of water have been poured over customers here for 300 years.

Street life along the busy promenade in between the crowded Galata Bridge and the old spice market is as rich as anywhere in the world. Pigeons on the steps of the Mosque, bus conductors and a travelling tea-bar. (RIGHT) Cathedral of cleanliness: the men's room at the Cagaloglu Hammam.

Rhodes Town

Senior citizens out for their morning strolls in the old town. Fortified by the Knights of St. John, and now invaded annually by a massive influx of tourists in the summer, its narrow twisted streets nonetheless remain little changed in 450 years.

Lindos

(TOP) Full sail on the Mediterranean beside the rocky coast of Rhodes.
(ABOVE & RIGHT) Lindos village: Mediterranean blue skies, fresh white walls and the hottest temperatures so far.

Paphos, Cyprus

Weddings and widows in a Cypriot village near Paphos: (ABOVE) One of the *blackbirds* – the widows of the village.

(ABOVE RIGHT) Traditional wedding: 3,000 guests, over-excited best man.

(RIGHT) Pin money: Bride and groom, adorned with banknotes from family and relatives, can make a considerable profit from the event.

Limassol, Cyprus

(LEFT) **In the wine country outside Limassol, after a hectic evening of demontrating her skills in a variety of dances, this young lady was crowned Miss Grape 1992. Her prize was 15 lbs (7kg) worth of chicken and one large fish.**

Port Said & Suez Canal

(TOP) **British holidaymakers negotiate the pontoon and the salesmen as they make their way into Africa for a 48-hour round trip from Cyprus to the Pyramids.** (MAIN PICTURE & RIGHT) **Egyptian holidaymakers by the Mediterranean: Port Said's fundamentalist Moslem administration forbids public sale of alcohol and women have to bathe fully clad. On the Suez Canal,** (RIGHT & BOTTOM) **fishermen seek Allah's blessing and his protection from the giant oil tankers.**

The Pyramids at Giza.
(TOP & RIGHT) Ships of the
Desert and their minders –
who would rather be
driving sports cars – wait
for their last load of
tourists before the sun
sets over the great
metropolis of Cairo
beyond. (LEFT) A mounted
official from the
Department of Antiquities
protects his Pyramid.

Valley of the Kings

83-year-old Tadorus, our guide, emerges into 40 degree heat from the tomb of Rameses III. 62 Pharaohs have been buried among these bare rock walls for 3,000 years. Forty have been discovered. Only one, the tomb of Tutankhamun, had not been looted.

Luxor

(OPPOSITE PAGE) Lounging beneath one of 134 three-thousand-year-old columns in the Hypostyle Hall, Karnak. Tadorus, my guide, was old enough to have been with Howard Carter when he discovered the Tutankhamun tomb in 1922. (ABOVE) Hieroglyphics, light and columns in Karnak. (LEFT ABOVE) Detail from a sarcophagus – a royal coffin. (LEFT) Whether on a ferry to the Valley of the Kings or on the road in Luxor, the way of life still belongs more to the Bible than the age of television.

As 96 per cent of the country is barren desert, all Egyptian life depends on the Nile. A thin strip of land on either side of the river was kept fertile by the annual flood. The Aswan Dam now prevents the flood, but they need chemicals to fertilise the land. (TOP LEFT & RIGHT) Feluccas remain the traditional river transport. (MIDDLE LEFT) A salesman works the captive audience as we wait to pass through the lock at Esna. They throw you the goods, you throw them the money.

Aswan

End of the Tourist Trail.

(RIGHT) The highest navigable point of the Nile. A series of cataracts and the massive walls of the Aswan Dam stop the tourist boats here.

(BELOW) The Cataract Hotel: last taste of luxury.

(BOTTOM) Farewell chorus from the rocks of Elephantine Island.

Aswan

(LEFT) On the four-lane Corniche by a river thick with feluccas and Nile cruisers laid up for lack of tourists, mother and child wait for their bus home.

WADI HALFA

Sudan

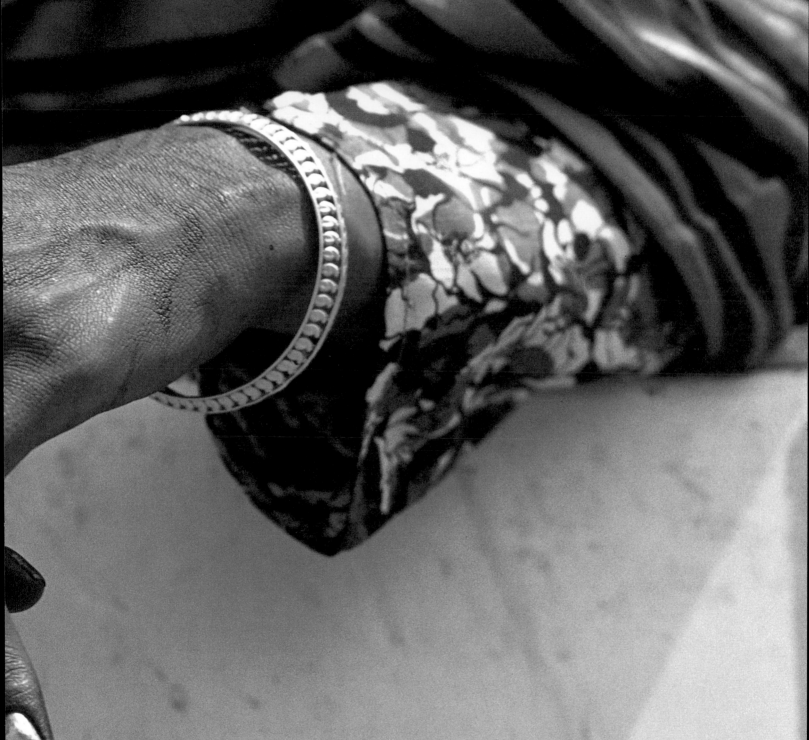

ASWAN

TROPIC OF CANCER

EGYPT

LIBYA

WADI HALFA

STATION 5
STATION 6

NUBIAN

DESERT

STATION 10   ABU HAMED   PORT SUDAN

SHEREIQ
5TH CATARACT

ATBARA

CHAD

SUDAN   SHENDI

OMDURMAN   KASSALA
KHARTOUM

WAD MEDANI

GEDAREF

GENEINA   GALLABAT   METEMA
                                                GONDAR
EN NAHUD   EL OBEID

NYALA   BAHIR DAR

WHITE NILE   BLUE NILE

MALAKAL

ETHIOPIA

WAU

CENTRAL AFRICAN
REPUBLIC

JUBA

LAKE
TURKANA

ZAIRE

UGANDA   KENYA
LAKE ALBERT

RED SEA

LAKE NASSER

GYPTIAN customs officials could not understand why we wanted to travel through the Sudan. Sudanese customs officials could not understand why we wanted to travel through Sudan. The Sudan is Africa's biggest country, and it has some of the biggest problems. We landed on a bone dry headland two or three miles (three to five kilometres) from the northern town of Wadi Halfa – stepping straight from the wide waters of Lake Nasser onto the sands of the Nubian desert. Somewhere beneath my feet was old Wadi Halfa, one of a score of towns and villages inundated when the waters of the Nile were spectacularly dammed at Aswan in the early 1970s. The Aswan High Dam, a tribute to Soviet-Egyptian co-operation, has meant little to Sudan except lost land and mass resettlement of the local Nubians, a thousand miles (1,600 kilometres) south. The new Nile Hotel in Wadi Halfa is a low, functional, concrete encampment surrounded by desert; the old Nile Hotel, Wadi Halfa, was one of a handsome succession of solid colonial buildings along a riverside corniche.

Wadi Halfa

The new Nile Hotel. Very dry, very hot and infinitely expandable. My thermometer hit 54 Celsius here. No guest was ever turned away, when the rooms were full, they slept in the corridors.

The grace and dignity of the local Nubians was immediately apparent. Generally tall and impressively handsome, their size belied a softness, a pleasure in smiling and a gentle, easygoing friendliness.

There is, I discovered, no such thing as a uniform, all-purpose Sudan. There are 270 tribes and languages betraying a much older, richer culture than the present boundaries, imposed by the colonial powers, might suggest, and which the present government would care to admit to.

The Nile Express

(TOP LEFT) **Coming down
after visiting Roof Class.
Most trains in Sudan carry
a crop of roof-riders. They
can travel free at their
own risk – which didn't
seem too great. There
were no bridges and the
trains never hit much
above 40 m.p.h. (70 k.p.h.)**
(TOP RIGHT) **Brief Encounter
at Wadi Halfa station.**

The fundamentalist government in Khartoum presented a perverse, cantankerous, severely anti-Western face – publicly allying themselves with Colonel Gaddafi, Saddam Hussein and the Soviet generals who had just imprisoned Gorbachev, prosecuting a fierce civil war against the Christians in the south and making life difficult for those few aid agencies who still had the time and patience to wrestle with the country's endemic problems of food shortage.

Wadi Halfa is a long way from anywhere. One single-track railway line, a quixotic relic of the old colonial days, connects this beleaguered northern outpost with Khartoum, but trains that used to run twice a week, now run once a month. It's quite an irony that this xenophobic government still keeps open a line built by Lord Kitchener's men in 1896 to move an army which destroyed their illustrious predecessor – Khalifa Abdullahi. Nor had they yet expunged the faded coat of arms and the peeling name of "The Nile Valley Express" on the threadbare coaches.

What *had* been removed were most of the internal fittings, leaving lavatories without basins and light sockets without bulbs, fan mountings without fans and door frames with nothing inside them.

The heat, though dry, was tremendous and when it cooled and sleep was possible for an hour or two, fine sand from the desert quickly lodged in nose, eyes and throat. There seemed to be no complaints. The train was a vast, peaceful community – the size of a small town, and I never once heard voices raised in anger. Even when one of the roof travellers fell asleep and rolled off into the desert, the driver simply stopped and reversed the train to pick him up.

The desert landscape was mesmerising: eerie, empty and compulsively watchable. I spent most of one night sitting at the door of the train looking out over mile upon mile of flat, duneless desert glowing in the moonlight.

The railway ran along by the Nile, now nearly 1,000 miles (1,600 kilometres) from where we had first seen it in Cairo, and as the discomfort began to outweigh the delights of the Nile Valley Express we switched to a bus for the last 100 miles (160 kilometres) from Atbara to Khartoum.

This was not a good idea. There were no roads in the desert and no springs on the vehicle. The combination was lethal. The faster we went, the greater was the chance of being impaled on the sharp metal fittings, by a driver who clearly didn't want us there anyway. We

survived somehow – to be rewarded with an arrival at Khartoum in the middle of a huge, enveloping sandstorm – a mighty cloud of dust and boiling wind from which we emerged, like minor prophets, at the glorious Valhalla of the Hilton Hotel.

If it was difficult to get into Khartoum, it was far harder to get out. An air of lassitude hung over the city. The government was positive about only one thing – we would under no circumstances be allowed to travel due south along the 30 degree line. The war in the south was severe enough to bar our way to Uganda and the Mountains of the Moon where the White Nile rises. We hung around, waiting for an alternative, and once the alternative had been found, permission to use it. We were to take the Blue Nile route, to the east.

Our saviours were a group of Eritreans who were able to take advantage of an extraordinary piece of luck. There might have been a civil war underway in Sudan, but in nearby Ethiopia, one had just ended. Though there were still rumours of bandits, peace had come to northern Ethiopia for the first time in 30 years. After some anxious and debilitating dog-days in Khartoum we received official permission to continue south east, across the Ethiopian border at Gallabat.

As with the rest of our progress through Sudan this was easier said than done. Vehicles broke down, late rains turned unmade roads into small canyons of hardening mud, slowing us to a crazy, sometimes perilous crawl. Hours became days and the border came no nearer. This, I eventually found out, was because no one knew where the border was.

None of our drivers had maps. If they did we would probably never have had to drive, head-down, through maize fields at all, nor would we have had to stop and ask anyone over the age of three where Ethiopia was, nor would we have had to spend the night in a police compound, kept awake by an unsleeping chorus of dogs, donkeys and other occupants of this fertile corner of south-east Sudan.

The name Gallabat became synonymous with the Promised Land, and when we eventually came across it, and found a collection of huts around a muddy, fetid border creek from which mosquitoes rose in a malarial swarm and a border bridge which was little more than tons of concrete poured into a stream we were idiotically relieved, and for some equally idiotic reason, thought the worst was over.

Khartoum

(FAR LEFT) **On my left... the Nile! And on my left... the Nile! Khartoum means** *Elephant's trunk*, **but the Nile not only bends here, it splits into two – Blue to Ethiopia, White to Uganda. (ABOVE) Beit el Khalifa: The house of Khalifa Abdullahi, the man defeated by Kitchener at the Battle of Omdurman in 1898, is now a museum of colonial relics. The steel boat is the one in which General Marchand made an audacious journey from the south to try and seize control of the Nile for France. Kitchener was extremely annoyed.**

Wadi Halfa

(ABOVE) Riding into the future on the back of a mule. Steel reinforcing rods pass through a shopping arcade of sticks and rags. The Nubians (RIGHT) are tall, graceful, gentle people. When the second Aswan Dam (the first was built by the British in 1902) was constructed, many were resettled 1,000 miles (1,600 kilometres) to the south. (LEFT) In the Sudan, as in all Arab countries, men hold hands quite unselfconsciously. (FAR LEFT) A protesting customer at the Wadi Halfa Customs shed. While (BELOW) Customs officers are clearly in no hurry.

Wadi Halfa

Nubian women. Under strict Islamic law women must wear a chador – a veil covering the head and body. There's nothing conformist about the colours, nor the expressions on the faces.

SUDAN

Nile Express

A small town on wheels.
4,000 passengers ride the
Kitchener Line in 50 degree
heat across the silent
sands of the Nubian
desert. Nearly 100 years
ago Egyptian and British
soldiers laid 230 miles
(370 kilometres) of track in
10 months. Even the train
doesn't go much faster
than this.

Nubian Desert

Away from the Nile, most of north Sudan is desert. (ABOVE) View from the bus-stop. On the Atbara – Khartoum service. Local head man, goat and, in background, distinctive and ancient conical tombs. The shop sold iced Pepsi – the desert equivalent of gold bars. (LEFT) In a poor country nothing is wasted. Railway sleepers become makeshift fences.

(TOP RIGHT) Camels are precious commodities. Here, at Omdurman camel market I was offered one for £1,000. The animals are immobilised in the

marketplace with one leg
pulled back and tied up.
(ABOVE) the shot that caused
a riot: Basil innocently
seeing only the beauty of
windblown veils, didn't
notice the huge civic dump
behind. Angry local men

attacked the car accusing
us of rubbishing the
Sudan. (RIGHT) Good
relations restored at
Omdurman market.
(OVERLEAF) Keeping cool
at the cattle market.

Sudan cannot afford much new technology. Their annual per capita income in 1988 was US$ 340. Switzerland's was US$ 27,260. Feluccas, the working boats of the Nile, are hand-built at Omdurman from a single trunk of wood (CENTRE LEFT) sawed lengthways (BOTTOM) into perfectly curved strips which make up the hull (LEFT). Even then, the whole process only takes 45 days.

(LEFT) Moving offices at the Ministry of Information: despite the strict religious and military regime, anyone could walk into the Ministry. But without their permission, a piece of paper, and several minders, it was impossible to walk much further than that. (BELOW) Pouffes are much sought after in the Sudan.

Omdurman

The Whirling Dervishes are
Moslems of the ascetic
Sufi sect, and they
perform every Friday
evening in front of the
Mosque of Hamed al Niel –
a sheikh credited with
miraculous powers.
Despite the frenzied
dancing as followers spin
themselves into an
ecstatic trance, it's quite
a genial occasion – anyone
in the family can join in.

Gedaref

On our way to the Ethiopian border we passed various roadside figures and a refugee camp (BELOW). Sudan, despite its own problems, is host to a million refugees. A self-appointed sergeant-major kept eager children at bay at this camp containing 22,000 "displaced" Ethiopians. The children had lived all their lives here.

Gedaref

Road to Gallabat

(ABOVE) On Sudanese roads it's best to stick to low-technology. (FAR LEFT) An up-ended truck in bandit country. He was carrying a cargo of salt up from Ethiopia. Now he's searching for his AA membership number. (LEFT) All-weather roads. Cattle die of thirst then (BELOW) rains arrive and turn the black soil into deep, mud-walled trenches.

M O Y A L E

SAUDI ARABIA

NUBIAN
DESERT

SUDAN

NILE

ERITREA

YEMEN

KASSALA

ASMERA

AL HUDAYDAH

GEDAREF

ADEN

GALLABAT   METEMA

BLUE NILE

GONDAR

LAKE TANA

DJIBOUTI

GULF OF ADEN

BAHIR DAR

DEBRE MARK'OS

DIRE DAWA

SOMALIA

HARER

AWASH

ADDIS ABABA

JIMA

ETHIOPIA

SHASHEMENE

LAKE AWASA

YIRGA ALEM

YABELO

LAKE TURKANA

MOYALE

MARSABIT

MOGADISHU

UGANDA

KENYA

INDIAN
OCEAN

LAKE VICTORIA

R E D   S E A

METEMA TO MOYALE

THE BORDER TOWN of Metema in Ethiopia was a mirror image of Gallabat. They faced each other across an open sewer that might once have been a stream or even a river. Sudan was poor, but Ethiopia was poorer. The civil war, between the centralised Marxist/Leninist dictatorship of Colonel Mengistu and the breakaway northern provinces of Tigray and Eritrea, had ended four months before we crossed the border, after almost 20 years of constant conflict. In the spring of 1991, the Tigrayan volunteer army had marched, virtually unopposed, through the country and into Addis Ababa. Though there was great rejoicing in the air, it could not disguise the underlying wretchedness of a country that since the mid-70s had spent over half its yearly earnings on fighting.

We grew accustomed to having armed guards in our vehicles, and to the depressing contradiction of poverty-stricken villagers in the midst of green, well-watered countryside. The old bore it stoically, the young, who had received no schooling for two or three years, were wide-eyed not with joy but with hunger, their protruding stomachs and fly-enclustered eyes showing how unfit they were to fight the diseases fed by lack of food.

By contrast the landscape on the way to Addis was glorious. Recent heavy rain had laid lush green gloss on the mountain pastures which sparkled with the brilliant yellow maskal flower – national emblem of Ethiopia. At the ancient capital city of Gondar, 7,000 feet (2,100 metres) above sea level, we reached the highest point of our journey so far.

Gallabat

Ethiopian Highlands: Tea at a border village with my teenage armed escort. They were a part of the world's youngest army, which had liberated Ethiopia from dictatorship only four months earlier.

105

Gallabat

(ABOVE) Sandbagged positions were never used. The government army surrendered with hardly a fight. Now the problem was what to do with half a million prisoners of war. (RIGHT) EPRDF (Ethiopian People's Revolutionary Democratic Front) soldier carries everything with him. (TOP LEFT) The daughter of Belai Berhe – a friend from Oxfam – in their Addis Ababa home.

From the relentless, unavoidable heat of the Sudan we found ourselves in the middle of an English autumn, with smoke rising from house fires, hailstones thudding from stormy skies, and eiderdowns in hotel bedrooms. The only similarity with the vast country we had just crossed was the complete lack of tourists, and in Ethiopia they were missing something. Gondar, a powerfully situated stronghold among the mountains, contains, in its centre, a cluster of castles dating from 1635. The architecture is an intriguing mixture of European and African styles. Like the rock-hewn churches of Lalibela, to the east, there is nothing remotely like them in the rest of Africa.

Spectacular scenery flanked the road all the way to Bahir Dar on the shores of Lake Tana. This extensive body of water stretches 50 miles (80 kilometres) to the north and there are at least 20 Christian monasteries secreted on its islands. Its magical remoteness is given an added significance for the Blue Nile rises here and, at this rainy season, an enormous volume of water rushed southwards to crash spectacularly over the rim of the giant waterfall at Tissisat.

Ethiopia is singular in many ways. It has its own calendar, about seven years behind our own. It was 1984 when we passed through. It is about the only African country that is unmarked by colonisation, having comprehensively defeated an attempted colonial occupation when the Italians were driven out after the Battle of Adowa in 1896. (Fortunately for us they returned in 1935, staying just long enough to build one of the best road networks in Africa.)

Ethiopia developed over the years as a feudal backwater, controlled by autocratic emperors and a powerful Christian church, largely out of sight of the rest of the world. Though Addis Ababa, which we reached after four days travel, contains a grand building or two, it's a very provincial capital. Most of the buildings have corrugated iron roofs, there were few cars, and Mengistu's attempt at anti-imperial aggrandizement was a series of tin-pot towers and triumphal arches the thickness of baked-bean cans. The fact that Ethiopia's exploiters were home-grown rather than European didn't seem to have made much difference. Subjugation has the same withering effect wherever it comes from. But there was, at last, in the summer of 1991, a tangible feeling of hope. The liberating Tigrayan army did not want to run the country, the relics of Mengistu's arrogance and excess were being pulled down and taken to rubbish tips, the new civilian government pledged itself to democracy, debate, discussion, a free press and

a revived economy. The rains had been generous and the worst of the famine had receded.

This, at any rate, was the buzz I got from talking to the crisp cotton-shirted "aidies" (aid-workers) who filled the foyer of the Hilton Hotel, hurrying past a display of the national coffee-making ceremony on their way to "Italian Night" at the buffet.

Before travelling south with a down-to-earth and dedicated Oxfam team, I took the opportunity to watch one of the most powerful forces in Ethiopian history at work – the Orthodox Church. I have never, and probably will never, see a ceremony quite like it. Enormous numbers of people attend – many more than can be accommodated inside. The church itself is built in a series of concentric circles around the Mak'das (the Holy of Holies) where the Tabot, a replica of the Ark of the Covenant, is accessible only to the priests. The playing of ancient instruments, like the sistrum and kebero drum, and the accompanying chanting, sounds more Hebrew than Christian – the opulent robes of the priests more like a high Catholic mass. The service is slow, powerful and remorseless.

From Addis we descended into the Great Rift Valley – a 4,000 miles (6,400 kilometres) split in the earth's crust running from Lebanon to Mozambique. The rich and elaborate rituals of the church stayed in my memory – a strong contrast to the plain mud and wattle huts and dying maize fields as we headed south. But here at least were successful crops of coffee and cotton, proving that Ethiopia, with help, has the potential to pull itself out of the present desperate state of disrepair. My memory of the country is confused. Splendid sights, great physical beauty, warm hospitality, the peculiar taste of the local rubbery bread called "injera", the uncomfortable sight of huge families hungry by the roadside, sensible Oxfam-funded local wells, crazy haphazard stripping away of tree-cover for fuel.

I wrote up all these impressions in my notebook at a hotel in the border town of Moyale as a column of ants scuttled across the page, and a tap dripped gently into the bucket that was my bathroom, shower, lavatory and wash-basin. It was hot and dry and there was much disease in this part of the country from tainted water. It seemed hellish at the time and yet Ethiopia, this big, backward, achingly beautiful country, was the first in Africa which I felt could also be Heaven on earth.

Addis Ababa

(TOP LEFT) A very ancient form of Christianity flourishes in a country surrounded by Moslem neighbours. The churches are richly decorated with glittery fabrics and (TOP RIGHT) a priest collects for church funds by the roadside. He upends his umbrella so passing motorists can contribute without stopping.

(ABOVE) The Blue Nile Gorge. Turning my back on the Nile for the last time, 2,500 miles (4,000 kilometres) south of Cairo.

North-Western Ethiopia is potentially very fertile. High mountains catch the rain and the scenery is in parts Alpine, but the long war had sucked the economy dry and the condition of the people was worse than anywhere else on our journey. But their spirit belied their circumstances and the foreigners' camera was a novelty.

Gondar

**Principal city of the
Highlands. Once the
capital of Ethiopia.
Palaces – like that of
Emperor Fasilidas, 1635,
(TOP LEFT) stand side by
side with poverty.
Surrounded by Moslem
neighbours, Ethiopia
remains predominantly
Christian since the first
conversions in 350 A.D.
Priests (LEFT) abound and
a Byzantine richness of
decoration (ABOVE) sits
incongruously in a world
of simple daub and
wattle houses.**

Lake Tana

One of the most precious stretches of water in the world. Lake Tana is not only the source of the Blue Nile but, it has been estimated, of 80 per cent of the water volume of Blue Nile and White Nile combined. The lake and the life that goes on around it has a sense of timelessness. Firewood is the chief commodity, shipped in ancient and precarious papyrus reed boats.

Blue Nile Falls

The Nile begins its life flowing towards the south and 19 miles (30 kilometres) south-west of Lake Tana plunges over a massive precipice at Tissisat – *Water that Smokes*. Heavy rains had swollen the flood to the greatest in living memory and water plunged off the basalt cliff with tremendous power. (LEFT) Wood is as important here as water. Weather can be cold in the mountains and large areas of the Highlands have been stripped of trees in the search for fuel, as well as fencing and building materials.

(LEFT) A *Sistrum*, an instrument unchanged since Biblical times hangs below a text written on skin in *Ge'ez*, ancient language of the priests.

(BELOW) In a small church next door to the palace, worshippers chanted and swayed to the rhythm of *Kebros* – large barrel-shaped drums – and *Sistra*, around the circular hallway which surrounded the inner core of the Holy of Holies.

Addis Ababa

The Church of St. Michael.
A service in the Ethiopian
Orthodox Church is
expected to last several
hours. Music and history
are vital ingredients of the
elaborate rituals which
have a distinctly Old
Testament flavour.
(BOTTOM RIGHT) Readings
from a 300-year-old Bible.
(LEFT) The entrance to
the Holy of Holies. Inside
is something only the
priests can touch –
a Tabot, replica of the
box that held the Ark
of the Covenant.

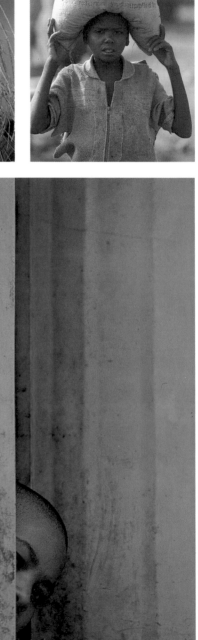

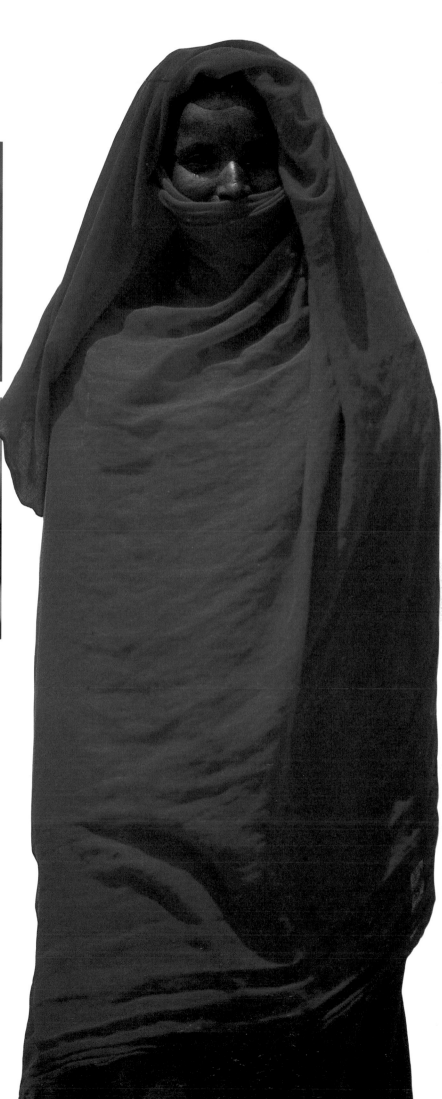

Ethiopian Faces

Country life is paraded along the roadsides. Children weave traditional straw headdresses. Everyone walks and the few commodities available are traded here, and carried away by head. 89 per cent of farming in Ethiopia is at subsistence level. Every member of the family is expected to lend a hand.

Evidence of the recent war often took the form of wall-paintings. Gruesome pictures of the hated Colonel Mengistu have been superseded by the peaceful, sober images of the new regime. Ethiopia's leader now is a 35-year-old lawyer – Meles Zenawi.

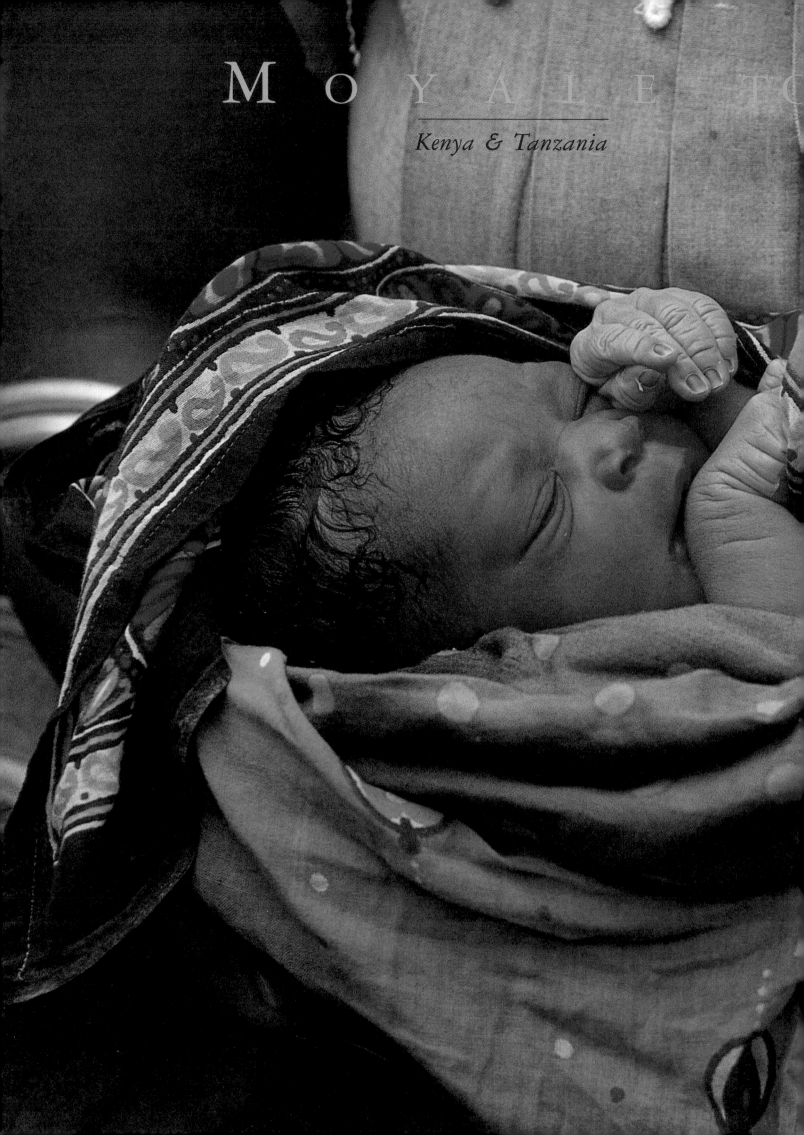

ETHIOPIA

WHITE NILE

ALBERT NILE

UGANDA

LAKE TURKANA

MOYALE

MARSABIT

KENYA

LAKE ALBERT

RIFT VALLEY

SHABA

LAKE KYOGA

EQUATOR

KAMPALA •

MT KENYA

LAKE EDWARD

LAKE VICTORIA

NAIROBI

MASAI MARA

RWANDA

LAMU

KIGALI •

MWANZA •

SERENGETI PLAIN

BURUNDI

NGORONGORO CRATER

ARUSHA

BUJUMBURA •

LAKE MANYARA

MOMBASA

KIGOMA

TANGA

UJIJI

TABORA •

LAKE TANGANYIKA

ZANZIBAR

DODOMA

INDIAN

MOROGORO • DAR-ES-SALAAM

OCEAN

LAKE RUKWA

TANZANIA

MPULUNGU

KILWA KIVINJE

LAKE MWERU

LINDI

ZAMBIA

MTWARA

KASAMA •

MASASI

RUVUMA

SHIWA NGANDU •

MALAWI

LAKE MALAWI

MUCHINGA MOUNTAINS

LUANGWA

MOZAMBIQUE

COMFORTABLE, colonial Kenya started badly. The Italian road-builders stopped at the Ethiopian border and we were 30 miles (50 kilometres) short of the Equator before we saw tarmac again. The dirt tracks of northern Kenya gave vehicles and passengers a battering. Two hours out of Moyale on the scrubby, featureless plain, a tyre hissed and expired. I sympathised. To make matters worse, we seemed as unsafe here as on the Sudan-Ethiopia border, with the authorities providing us with an armed escort in case of attack by Somali irregulars.

Marsabit rose to the occasion – a green and fertile mountain plateau, affording striking views of volcanic craters, our first real glimpses of wildlife, and a cool respite from the hot dust of the desert floor. I had seen glorious birds like the Goliath Heron and the African Fish Eagle beside the lakes of Ethiopia, but most of the wild animals of Ethiopia had been hunted to extinction and it was only at Marsabit that I experienced the excitement of seeing huge creatures emerge from dense, unfamiliar forest and move to within a hundred yards (90 metres) of me to take water and, in the case of the elephants, rub themselves ecstatically in the dust.

Having negotiated the remote and inhospitable northern desert of Kenya, the route south took us rudely, if temporarily, back to a predictable, western-influenced world. The roadside firewood and sweetcorn sellers of Southern Ethiopia were replaced by jewellery salesmen – hard, persistent characters, wits sharpened by a new kind of demand. We were back on the tourist trail. Striped buses with open-topped roofs ferried rich visitors round the wildlife reserves, and when the day was done they could relax back into big, fat armchairs at the Mount Kenya Country Club. We crossed the Equator beside an electricity sub-station. In Nairobi

Marsabit

(ABOVE) **After a long hard drive through Dida Galgalu – the *Plains of Darkness*, we arrived in Marsabit – the *Place of Cold*, covered in red dust.** (PRECEDING PAGES) **A baby girl born in the restaurant car of the Dar-Es-Salaam to Kigoma Express. Easily the best thing they produced on the journey.**

Masai Mara

Early rising beside the Mara River. Animal-spotting begins at dawn. On my *Out of Africa* safari about the only thing that wasn't provided was someone to shave me.

we waited at pedestrian crossings for a crocodile of blazered and beribboned schoolgirls, in matching pink and grey uniforms.

Nairobi was the nearest to normality that we'd seen for many weeks – traffic jams, pollution, drug problems and political corruption. It was just like home.

Without much protest we surrendered for a few days to the blandishments of an Abercrombie and Kent "Out of Africa" tented safari. We didn't have to actually put up the tents, someone else took care of that; we didn't have to actually boil our shaving water or cook over a camp fire – someone else took care of that; we certainly didn't have to shoot anything – other than me watching lions mating or having my shaving water boiled, or my food cooked by someone else.

I fell asleep each night to the sound of hippos gurgling, spluttering and gasping uproariously, only a few feet away in the Mara River. I found their exclamations rather comforting (I was told that hippo sounds are by no means arbitrary and that these often absurd eruptions were part of a "hippo language" consisting of over 100 separate grunts). I liked it least when I woke in the depths of the night and heard nothing at all. This is when the hippos emerge from the water and take to the river banks. I was told of one which, startled whilst inside the camp, stampeded away through the kitchen tent, and plunged off across the plain with it wrapped around his head. There was a lot of comedy out there in the wild. I particularly liked seeing warthogs reversing into their holes in the ground and male ostriches' legs turning pink before mating. Now I know why we invented trousers.

The brief idyll amongst the animals continued into northern Tanzania, where the remains of the great migratory herds of wildebeest could still be seen, plodding home across the Serengeti plains from the grasslands of Kenya and providing lion, leopard and cheetah with regular meals on the way. This was the territory of the Masai, originally tribal relatives of the colourful, fashion-conscious Samburu in northern Kenya. The tourist-conscious Masai wore equally fine jewellery and interesting costume but, judging by the herdsmen we encountered on the rim of the Ngorongoro Crater, were more adept at making money from it.

Tanzania had a different feel. For many years they had pursued a non-aligned economic policy, though the Chinese had built them a railway. Despite having a greater

proportion of national parkland than any other country in Africa, and extraordinary natural beauties like Mount Kilimanjaro and the Ngorongoro Crater, it is not easy to find good accommodation or transport in the country much beyond a hundred miles (160 kilometres) of the Kenyan border. We drove hard, fast and uncomfortably to Dodoma, the tiny capital city in the middle of nowhere. From here, with the help of the Dar-Es-Salaam Express and a line originally built by German colonialists, we were able to complete our semi-circular detour round southern Sudan and end up, tired but cautiously triumphant, at Kigoma – like Leningrad, Kiev, Odessa and Cairo – on 30 degrees East.

I t has to be said that the similarities ended there, for Kigoma is not one of the world's great cities, nor was the Railway Hotel the Ritz. My mosquito net had holes big enough for a warthog to reverse through, the "High-Style" (i.e. Western) lavatories were awaiting supplies of seats, the hot-water pipes were there, but not connected to the water-supply and the concept of fast-food or even reasonably quick food had not reached the shores of Lake Tanganyika.

Lake Tanganyika is Kigoma's greatest asset. It's a long, deep waterway, stretching 420 miles (670 kilometres) through the heart of Africa. A 77-year-old German-built ferry boat, the M.V. *Liemba*, turned out to be our lifeline, running a unique service down the Tanzanian coast to the north Zambian port of Mpulungu.

Unless you made friends with the Captain, conditions on board could be pretty grim, but there was plenty to see en route. We passed the historic little town of Ujiji where Stanley eventually tracked down Livingstone, and 15 more stops provided a regular series of mini-dramas. There is no navigational chart of the lake and, as Captain Beatus T. Mghamba did not want to venture too near the coast, all incoming and outgoing passengers, goods, parcels, letters, babies, brides and bridegrooms had to be transferred by ferry to and from the shore. At every one of the 15 stops an unruly armada would race out to the *Liemba*, jostling fiercely and quite ruthlessly for a position alongside. The scenes made Tokyo at rush-hour look like a class in Zen Buddhism.

Then, quite suddenly, no one was left on board, except ourselves and a handful of Zambian businessmen returning to their country to vote in the election. Tanzania slipped away astern, the forbiddingly high cliffs of Zaire loomed on the port aside but ahead of us, nestling alluringly between low wooded hills, was Mpulungu, Zambia, and the start of Southern Africa.

Kigoma

(ABOVE) Boarding the M.V. *Liemba,* which remains, after 77 years of service on Lake Tanganyika, the only regular passenger ship for people travelling between Kigoma, Mpulungu and the 15 coastal villages in-between.

Moyale

Some of the first Kenyans we encountered after crossing the border at Moyale. In Africa, women are the carriers and gatherers. Boys tend the camel herds. Men keep a low profile.

North Kenya

The long dirt-road south to Marsabit. War-torn Somalia was only a hundred miles (160 kilometres) away and the Kenyans insisted we travel with an armed escort. We saw no soldiers, only victims of the hard times. These women wanted water more than food.

100 miles (160 kilometres) from the Equator we reached Samburu country. The tribes are a branch of the Ma people, distant relatives of the more famous Masai in the south. Their name means *Butterfly* and they love dressing up. Jewellery and adornment is much-prized.

Lerata

(ABOVE) Inside the Shaba National Reserve, 160 miles (260 kilometres) from Marsabit, a group of young warriors preen themselves by the river. Instead of their spears, they use stones against tourists who pry with their video cameras and long lenses. Their aim is deadly accurate. (BELOW) A man's wealth lies in the number of cattle he owns, but years of low rainfall have made it hard to keep them and wells like this are becoming overcrowded.

Masai Mara

Life in the wild is not always discreet. (FAR LEFT) A lioness carries the runt of her litter of four who's having trouble keeping up. (LEFT) A wildebeeste dinner for a pride of lions. There's a strict pecking order – men first, boys last. (RIGHT) Giraffe look awkward but move with mesmerising grace. (BELOW) Mara River – balloonist's-eye-view of my safari home.

Mara River

Night falls at our
encampment in the middle
of the Masai Mara. The
hippo chorus quietens and
they emerge from the river
at dead of night. The
night-watchman, who
stays up to make sure
they stay out of our tents,
builds a fire to keep
away the damp chill of the
Mara River.

Ngorongoro

The world's second largest crater; a massive disc in the Rift Valley – 12 miles (20 kilometres) wide and 1,970 feet (600 metres) deep. Still in Masai territory.

Kigoma Express

No one bothers to use the restaurant car, all the food is carried or bought, ready-cooked. At almost every station, there is a feast laid out on the platform – fried fish, kebabs, chicken stews, rice and beans. Live animals were also available. (FAR RIGHT) Wood for sale; a recurring image of Africa. Children doing the work again.

Ujiji

Where Livingstone and
Stanley met in 1871. At
one-time, a thriving centre
of the slave-trade, now
boat-builders and
fishermen fill the beaches.
When they are not helping
out with chores, the
children (LEFT) show
remarkable inventiveness,
keeping themselves
entertained with little
more than sticks and
wires.

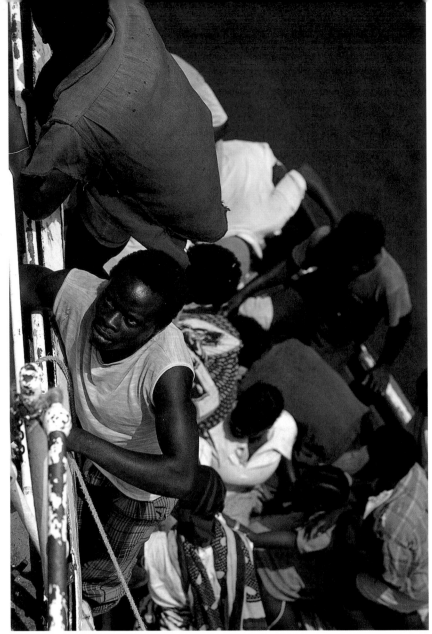

Lake Tanganyika

Lack of navigation maps prevented the *Liemba* from going inshore. Passengers came out to us. Hundreds of people poured on and off the ship; climbing over, under and through the railings during the 15 rush hours of the journey. (RIGHT) A floating wedding party tries to get aboard.

CAPE TOWN

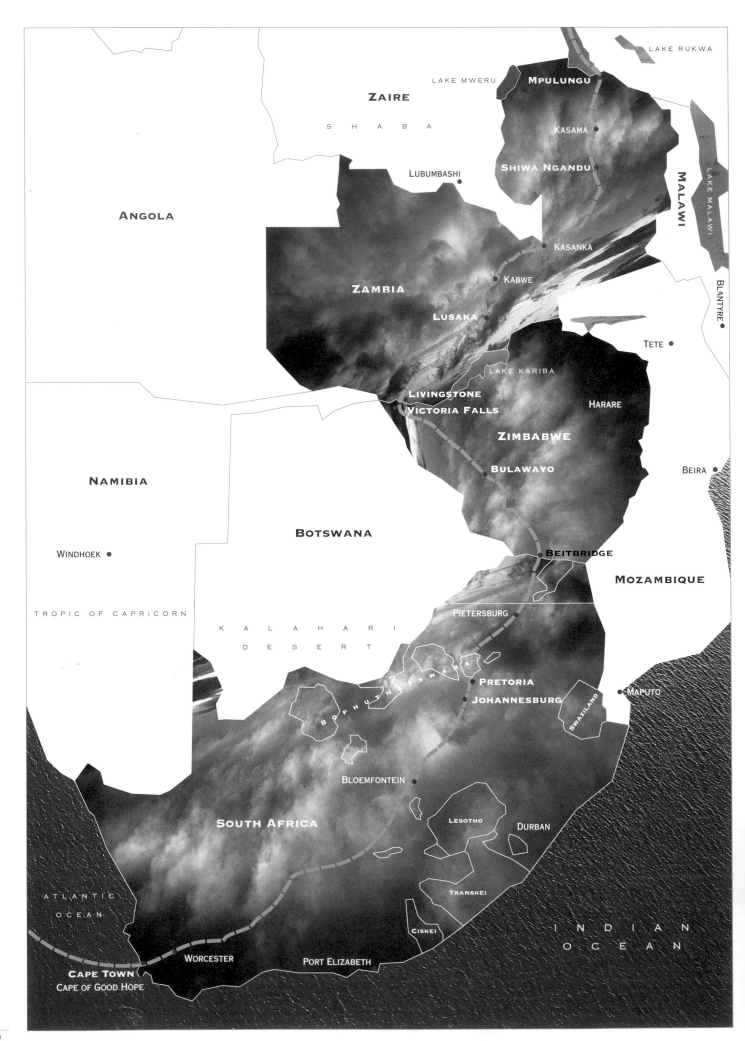

LAKE RUKWA

ZAIRE

LAKE MWERU

MPULUNGU

SHABA

KASAMA

MALAWI

LUBUMBASHI

SHIWA NGANDU

LAKE MALAWI

ANGOLA

BLANTYRE

KASANKA

ZAMBIA

KABWE

LUSAKA

TETE

LAKE KARIBA

LIVINGSTONE

VICTORIA FALLS

HARARE

NAMIBIA

ZIMBABWE

BEIRA

BULAWAYO

BOTSWANA

BEITBRIDGE

MOZAMBIQUE

WINDHOEK

TROPIC OF CAPRICORN

PIETERSBURG

KALAHARI

DESERT

BOPHUTHATSWANA

PRETORIA

MAPUTO

JOHANNESBURG

SWAZILAND

BLOEMFONTEIN

LESOTHO

DURBAN

SOUTH AFRICA

TRANSKEI

ATLANTIC

OCEAN

CISKEI

INDIAN

OCEAN

WORCESTER

PORT ELIZABETH

CAPE TOWN

CAPE OF GOOD HOPE

I HAD SOMEHOW expected Southern Africa to be a return to the familiar. After all this was the land of Cecil Rhodes and Jan Smuts, of Rorke's Drift and Mafeking, of ranches and plantations and gold mines. After the deserts and civil wars of the north and the hot plains and remote settlements of Central Africa, this was to be the easy bit. So I confidently thought as I entered Zambia, one hundred and eight days into the journey. By day one hundred and nine all my expectations had been thoroughly shaken up. On the day we reached the hot and sticky dockside at Mpulungu, the Zambians went to the polls and I went to see a witch-doctor. There were fairly drastic effects in both cases. For President Kaunda, it meant losing office for the first time in the 18 years since he led Zambia to independence, for me it meant a string of minor disasters that made me question for the first time whether it was possible to complete the journey.

In a different part of Mpulungu that day, away from the docks and the fish factory and the tree-shaded rondavels of the small hotel a "healer" from Zaire was at his surgery among the straw-thatched huts of the native village.

It was an opportunity to meet, for the first time in Africa, what we westerners would call a witch-doctor. Dr. Baela certainly looked the part, but any tendency to dismiss him as a ridiculous outdated figure was

Mpulungu

(ABOVE) **I first learn of my evil spirits – Dr. Baela's surgery. Mpulungu, Zambia.**

tempered by the absolute belief shown in him by a crowd of two or three hundred villagers who crowded round in rapt concentration, to hear his consultation with me.

Dr. Baela smoked a very large cigarette and stared deep into my soul through blood-shot eyes. He told me, through a translator, that I had an evil spirit and that I would lose all my money and that the journey ahead would be very dangerous for me unless I rid myself of the spirit. The medicine he prescribed was a strip of tree-bark, which he advised me to cut, grind into powder, cover my body with and wash off, in a private place, before sticking the remainder of the powder up my nose.

I thanked Dr. Baela, took the bark and returned to a more comfortable life. Except that it was no longer comfortable. That night my body was racked with the worst pain of the journey. I recovered a little as I was driven south in one of the huge fish delivery trucks which take the produce of Lake Tanganyika to the tables of Zimbabwe and South Africa. I felt bad enough to have to forego much of the generous hospitality at Shiwa estate, where John and Lorna Harvey, later tragically killed in the south of Zambia, put us up for a day or two. Then Patti Musicaro, the camera assistant, was diagnosed as having caught malaria. For the first time things seemed to be falling apart.

Without further hesitation I searched for Dr. Baela's bark and, using my Swiss army knife, cut it, ground it into powder, covered my body with it and washed, in a private place beside a hippo-filled lake in Kasanka National Park, before placing generous amounts of the rest up each nostril. I sneezed for about 45 minutes but slept without discomfort for the first night in ages.

Perhaps I should have taken a bigger dose, for far from improving, things got worse.

Whilst white-water rafting in the Zambesi I was sucked under the water and cracked a rib against a submerged rock. I limped back to the hotel only to find that one of my two travelling bags had been lost, believed stolen, on the journey down from Lusaka.

The spirit of Dr. Baela seemed to have pursued me through Zambia, but at least there was now nothing more I could do about it. His tree-bark was in the stolen bag.

Though I liked the Zambians for their affability and unflappability in the face of a crackpot economy and declining services, I was relieved to cross the Zambesi Bridge, un-scathed. But only just. A party of New Zealanders tried to interest me in joining them in what they claimed was the first ever Bungee jump in Africa. Flinging myself off the bridge

into a 660-foot (200-metre) abyss, tied only by my ankles to a length of elastic rope, did not seem a sensible thing for an ex-patient of Dr. Baela.

Zimbabwe, which won independence eight years later than Zambia, after a bitter civil war, was much more reminiscent of Britain. Indeed the hospital at Victoria Falls at which my cracked rib was diagnosed was smarter all round than any I'd seen at home. A gleaming train, still bearing the 'RR' – Rhodesian Railways -- mark on the windows, ran on time into the English suburban atmosphere of Bulawayo, with its bowling greens and manicured parks and department stores sprouting Christmas trees as summer approached. Ninety years after his death, the spirit of Cecil Rhodes, the great capitalist, still hangs over a country led by a Marxist, Robert Mugabe. His private train is faithfully preserved in Bulawayo and his remains lie ringed by massive granite boulders in the nearby Matobo Hills.

We were impatient to be in Cape Town now, after 10 weeks of travelling and recording in Africa and, thankfully, our fortunes improved. Once across the Limpopo and into the Republic of South Africa, we drove on the best roads we'd yet seen in Africa, through the first mountain range we'd seen since Ethiopia, to Johannesburg. Though the city had all the mod-cons, the diametrically opposed circumstances of most whites and most blacks made this one of the more melancholy stops. The gold mines have created massive yellow spoil heaps around the city and with the prospect of employment lured millions of blacks away from the countryside and into drab, poorly-serviced townships. But times are changing in South Africa and in Soweto I was able to visit a family we got to know in London, who had only, in the extraordinary summer of 1991, been allowed back to the country where they were born and which had kept them out for 30 years for belonging to the ANC.

The Blue Train, privilege enshrined in transport, made the last 900 miles (1,450 kilometres) of Africa the most comfortable of all and the sight of the great travel icon of Table Mountain marking the end of the continent, and the warm, clear sunshine of the Cape raised all our spirits.

But I still couldn't entirely forget the other sort of spirits, the ones Dr. Baela warned me of in Mpulungu. Could they be in any way responsible for the news that there was, after all, no room for us on the South African supply ship to Antarctica? And if we did find another way to the South Pole, would they come along there too?

Bulawayo

(LEFT) Aboard Cecil Rhodes' private train, 90-years-old and better preserved than I was by then. (TOP RIGHT) Great Doormen of the World – The Victoria Falls Hotel, Zimbabwe. (ABOVE) On top of Table Mountain, Cape Town. After the bad news of our ship, the Antarctic never seemed so far away.

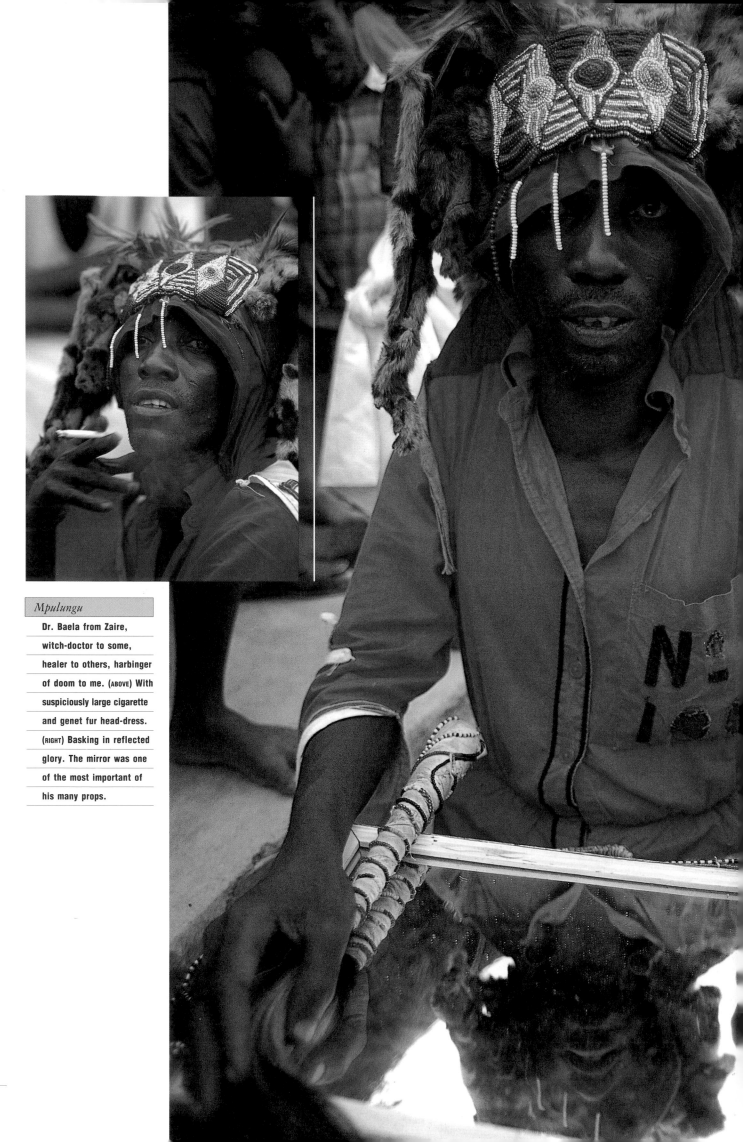

Mpulungu

Dr. Baela from Zaire, witch-doctor to some, healer to others, harbinger of doom to me. (ABOVE) With suspiciously large cigarette and genet fur head-dress. (RIGHT) Basking in reflected glory. The mirror was one of the most important of his many props.

Mpulungu

(LEFT) A ritual exorcism in progress: like an out of control school play. The white-robed man in welding goggles is Baela's assistant. Others in white robes are his young acolytes. The shirtless figure is a man suspected of murder. His skin is slashed and live chickens held above him to summon out the sprits. (ABOVE) The robes and head-dresses make these heathen practices look like scenes from the Old Testament.

Zambia

Roadside wares come in all shapes and sizes, as do the salesmen – boys with bananas, sticks and bags of charcoal. Timber provides shelter, building materials and fuel, and much of the woodland we passed had been stripped and burned to keep up with demand.

(RIGHT) Missing the train.

Victoria Falls

Nothing had prepared me for
the splendours of what the
locals call Musi-o-Tunya,
The Smoke That Thunders.
The deceptively aimless
Zambesi River suddenly
cascades 250 feet
(76 metres) over a cliff
and is flung down a series
of rapids that only a fool
would attempt to ride.
*(See overleaf for fool
in action.)*

Victoria Falls

My first experience of total immersion since the baptisms in Russia. Somewhere inside the Zambesi River, myself and a dozen companions are having the time of our lives. There is no way of adequately explaining the appeal of white-water rafting. It's just that every now and then it seems important for us to do something very stupid. I survived (ABOVE) but with a cracked rib.

Bulawayo

**Bulawayo on the move.
Coal on the steam-engines,
tyres on the roads, plants
on the streets and white
skirts on the greens of the
B.B.C. – the Bulawayo
Bowls Club.**

Bulawayo

Night moves at the legendary Umtshitshimbo Beer Garden. (RIGHT) Thandeka Ngoro, diva of the dance-halls, adds vocal power to a band led by Steve Dyer, a white South African. (LEFT) Bulawayo's businessmen go wild.

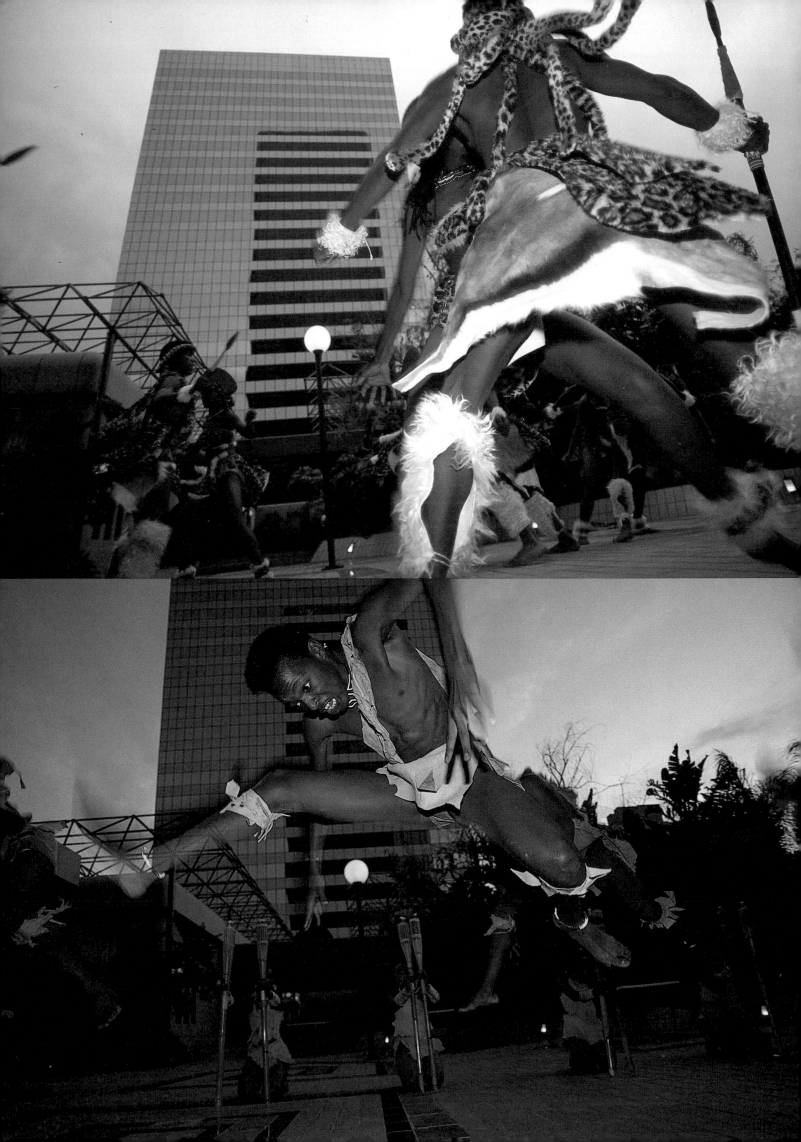

Soweto

The *victims*, as our guide called these shanty town dwellers in Mandela Village, lured in from the countryside by the prospect of work which never comes. They take pride in surviving in huts which are put up overnight. There is no regular sanitation or school for the children. (PRECEDING PAGES) Multi-racial culture: A modern dance company from Soweto perform at a downtown Johannesburg hotel. It's a long way from Rorke's Drift.

Western Deep Mines

South Africa's most durable asset: (TOP) The moment the face workers never see. The crucible tips to reveal gold for the first time. Each ingot is worth around £150,000. (BELOW) The face workers: teams of three men per drill, working bent double at 30 Celsius for six hours a shift. And they're the lucky ones, the highest paid of the manual workers. (OVERLEAF) South Africa from behind the glass. The Blue Train from Pretoria to Cape Town.

Cape Town

(RIGHT) Table Mountain combines with Signal Hill, the Lion's Head and the Twelve Apostles to form the spectacular amphitheatre of rock which encircles one of the world's great natural harbours. It had taken us almost 80 days to cross Africa from Mediterranean to Atlantic.

Cape of Good Hope

(ABOVE) The end of Africa.
The Cape of Good Hope. In
our case it didn't quite
live up to its name.

SANTIAGO TO

Chile & Antarctica

S O U T H   P O L E

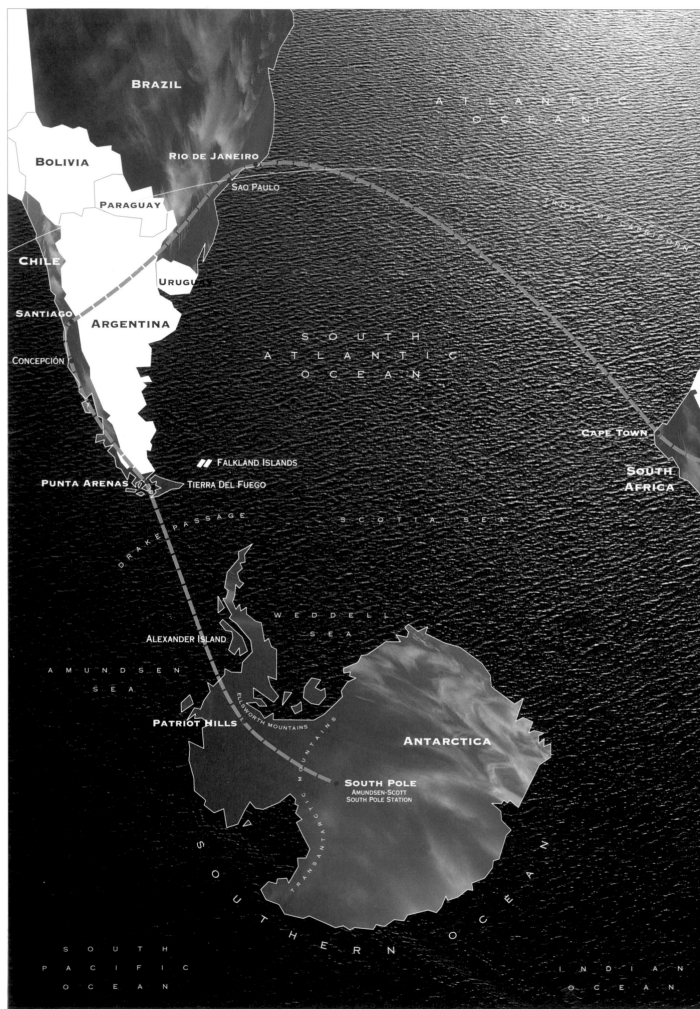

BRAZIL

BOLIVIA

RIO DE JANEIRO

ATLANTIC
OCEAN

PARAGUAY

SAO PAULO

TROPIC OF CAPRICORN

CHILE

URUGUAY

SANTIAGO

ARGENTINA

SOUTH
ATLANTIC
OCEAN

CONCEPCIÓN

CAPE TOWN

FALKLAND ISLANDS

SOUTH
AFRICA

PUNTA ARENAS

TIERRA DEL FUEGO

SCOTIA SEA

DRAKE PASSAGE

WEDDELL
SEA

ALEXANDER ISLAND

AMUNDSEN
SEA

PATRIOT HILLS

ELLSWORTH MOUNTAINS

ANTARCTICA

TRANSANTARCTIC MOUNTAINS

SOUTH POLE
AMUNDSEN-SCOTT
SOUTH POLE STATION

SOUTHERN OCEAN

SOUTH
PACIFIC
OCEAN

INDIAN
OCEAN

VOLTAIRE must have known a thing or two about Polar travel when he said in *Candide*, *"All is for the best in the best of possible worlds."* He certainly knew enough not to bother going there at all. But if he had had to, he would have known that getting there is essentially a pragmatic business. The great white wastes are no place for the idealist. Which, I suppose, is why Scott was second and Amundsen first. Scott, with his horses and his hang-ups, dragging the weight of class, empire and national destiny across the ice and into the teeth of the ferocious winds that seem to blow for ever from the bottom of the earth.

Whereas the North Pole is in the middle of the ocean, surrounded by land, the South Pole is in the middle of land surrounded by ocean. The nearest town is Punta Arenas, 1,700 miles (2,740 kilometres) away, further from the South Pole than Helsinki, Stockholm and Oslo are from the North.

Average temperatures at the South Pole, far away from the warming ocean, are as low as minus 55 Celsius all year round. The Pole itself sits on a block of ice 6,600 feet (2,000 metres) thick, and 9,900 feet (3,000 metres) above sea level.

Though I was assured by Americans at the Amundsen-Scott Base that they knew of people who had been photographed naked at the Pole, all I can say is they must have used the fastest film, for to expose any part of the body to the relentless and aching polar wind is painful.

Nuclear submarines and Russian ice-breakers can trundle up to, over, under and around the *top* of the world whenever they want but to get to 90 degrees South requires a different kind of commitment. Perhaps it was for the best that we found our Pole to Polar progress temporarily halted at Cape Town, for instead of relying on a scientific supply vessel, we found ourselves in the hands of the only tour operator in the world to specialise

Patriot Hills

If you've ever owned a globe, then I'm standing on the bit at the bottom that no one ever dusts. It was high summer when the picture was taken at the Patriot Hills. Daytime temperatures rose to freezing point.

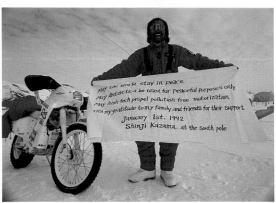

Patriot Hills

(TOP) **Mike Sharp, station manager, keeps in touch with some of the 80 scientific stations in Antarctica. 20 nations are represented, including India and Poland.**

(ABOVE) **Kazama-San and the message he hopes to motorbike to the Pole.**

(CENTRE) **Sastrugi: Sharp wind-blown ice-ridges provide the runway for our take-off to the Pole.**

in the interior of the Antarctic. They didn't come cheap, but one of the hidden benefits of our rough and ready travelling across Africa was that we had enough money left in the bank to uproot ourselves from the beaches of Cape Town and fly 6,000 miles (9,600 kilometres) to the mountains of Chile, first to Santiago, the capital, and from there to a town at the end of the Andes called Punta Arenas.

Here we joined a group of some 20 other adventurers – mountaineers from New Zealand, including the son of the first man to the top of Everest, a burly Japanese who wanted to be the first man (and later was) to reach the South Pole on a motor cycle, an Australian doctor who wanted to climb the highest mountain in the Antarctic, and a quiet middle-aged American with a lot of money who had done the North Pole earlier in the year and now wanted to do the South. I was tempted to write this off as the silliest reason of all until of course I remembered he and I were after exactly the same thing.

In Punta Arenas the elements of the final drama were assembled and duly began to unfold. In the incongruously soft-furnished surroundings of a hotel lounge we were given dire warnings about what to look forward to in the southern continent – the burning power of the sun on the ice, the sudden, violent changes in weather which make it imperative never to leave camp alone, the shortage of oxygen high up at the Pole itself, and above all the constant wind making it necessary to tie down gloves, hats and any other accessories.

Out on the runway a 40-year-old DC-6 waited for a break in the weather. The pilot studied weather charts which showed a pattern of depressions like spots on a leopard. It was not good. When the word came that the time was right for the 1,700 miles (2,700 kilometres) flight I had mixed emotions. I knew I had to finish the journey but, worn down by the nagging discomfort of a cracked rib and 138 days on the road, I knew also that I was not as fit as I should be – certainly not as fit as the Australians and New Zealanders, fresh from home. The moment when our DC-6 flew away from South America, leaving behind rain-soaked green fields the colour of the Yorkshire moors beside which I was born, I felt very clearly that I was tempting fate, quite outrageously. I just hoped fate would understand.

From that point on the sheer excitement of what I was seeing seemed to inject new life and enthusiasm. 10,000 feet (3,000 metres) below us the first icebergs flecked the rough waters of the Drake Passage. As we came in towards the land-mass itself the icebergs grew in size until, like a film run backwards, they merged into a mass of shattered blocks and floes and

ice-cliffs which in turn became one sheet of white. The occasional black triangle of mountain-top broke through, showing that we were now over Antarctica, a land-mass one and a half times the size of the United States of America.

This was still only the first act of the drama, which ended with a test of nerves as our DC-6 hit the blue-ice runway at Patriot Hills and we were swung and slid onto the surface of the continent, throttle shrieking and surrounding snow whipped into a mini-blizzard.

In the tents at Patriot Hills, a series of red smudges on a vast, silent, white canvas, we enjoyed a domestic interlude, a brief and unreal few days of stew and reading and Chilean red wine as, once again, the weather situation, in the last 600 miles (960 kilometres) between us and the Pole, tightened the tension. Could we or couldn't we? Should we or shouldn't we?

It was hard to concentrate on anything other than the crackling of the radio set as the various remote stations that provide the only human presence on Antarctica, compared notes on weather and conditions. When the news came of settled conditions over the Pole, the adventure reached its final, slightly absurd climax. There was nothing very glamorous about the last 600 miles (960 kilometres). There was only a single engine on the aircraft selected to get us there. Dan, the pilot, was an old timer quite un-fazed by anything, including the fact that neither he, nor the plane he was flying had ever been to the Pole before.

"We'll find it," he grinned, slamming shut the cockpit door which had a heart-stopping habit of falling open in mid-air.

As if Steven Spielberg had written the story, we even had to put down between Patriot Hills and the Pole in order to dump fuel for the Japanese motorcyclist's later attempt. Dan left us in a tent on the ice 300 miles (480 kilometres) from nowhere, as he flew the fuel into place. Never have two hours passed so slowly.

It was 1.15 in the morning, South American time, when I first caught sight of the South Pole. My childhood hero, Captain Scott, had seen something which chilled what was left of his unchilled blood when he came here almost 80 years ago – a pile of stones and a Norwegian flag. A little of his depression rubbed off on me when I saw the tractors, diggers, mobile homes, oil-drum stacks, and spare-part depots which mark the modern South Pole. The last place on earth had been colonised and an American flag marked the end of my five and a half month journey.

The combination of cold, lack of sleep and altitude sickness made the last few steps take for ever. I've rarely felt worse, but there I am in the photo, smiling like the day I was born. I was standing on the South Pole. That was all that mattered.

Santiago

(FAR LEFT) Fleeing rudely from one continent to another, I ask for blessing from the virgin of Santiago. Sadly she was closed.

(ABOVE) Working the fish at the Mercado Central. From a coastline of 2,500 miles (4,000 kilometres), Chilean fish is plentiful, unusual and can be tasted on the spot at fine restaurants in the market itself.

(LEFT) Our sound-man, Fraser Barber, wins the fashion battle with the Presidential Guard.

Into Antarctica

(LEFT) The 40-year-old DC-6 is fuelled for the 1,700 miles (2,700 kilometres) flight.

(TOP LEFT & ABOVE) 1,000 miles (1,600 kilometres) in. Over pack ice in the Bellingshausen Sea. Icebergs, some many miles across, calving off the ice-shelf. (FAR LEFT) First sight of the Antarctic continent. Foreground, a crescent of Nunataks – the peaks of mountains submerged beneath an ice-sheet up to 13,000 feet (4,000 metres) deep. In the background, the Ellsworth Mountains contain the continent's highest peak Mount Vinson – 16,863 feet (5,140 metres).

(ABOVE) Nearly nine hours flying time from Punta Arenas, the DC-6 makes a blue-ice landing at the Patriot Hills. The pilot couldn't use any brakes – he only had the ice and the throttle to play with. This type of landing was only pioneered in the last ten years.

South Pole

Five and a half months since setting out I reached the last place on earth – the South Pole, 90 degrees South, 9,180 feet (2,800 metres) above sea level. Minus 57 Celsius in the wind. And it's the middle of the night. I wish I could say I was on the spot where Amundsen once stood, but the ice cap moves some 32 feet (10 metres) every year, hence the line of marker flags behind me indicating South Poles of the past.

(LEFT) The reason for the Stars and Stripes is that only the Americans had the money to build a permanent base here. It's called the Amundsen-Scott South Pole Station and it's dug into the ice. 100 scientists work here in summer, 20 in the long, dark, bitterly cold winter.